Russel Subayi Mbaya

The 3 Effective Steps to Rebuild Your Life

Russel Subayi Mbaya

The 3 Effective Steps to Rebuild Your Life

Making peace with one's past, Update his state of mind, Feeding one's hunger

Éditions Vie

Imprint

Cover image: www.ingimage.com

Publisher:
Éditions Vie
is a trademark of
International Book Market Service Ltd., member of OmniScriptum Publishing Group
17 Meldrum Street, Beau Bassin 71504, Mauritius

Printed at: see last page
ISBN: 978-613-9-58956-2

The 3 Effective Steps to Rebuild Your Life

This book talks about three important principles that can help a person rebuild their life as part of their personal development.

Whether we find ourselves in a situation where we have experienced the death of a loved one, divorce, the break-up of a love relationship, the loss of a job, or starting a new life in a host country, we need to rebuild ourselves and move forward.

In order to rebuild one's life for whatever reason, it is imperative to make **peace with one's past, to update one's state of mind, and finally to feed one's appetite.**

The author himself, at one point in his life, found himself in a situation where he had to rebuild his life from top to bottom. Here he gives the secrets of the principles that helped him to make this journey and move forward.

Discover anew the wonders that happen with the power of positive thinking, time management, and the importance of being independent in all aspects of one's personal life.

Acknowledgements

My thanks go straight to all those who have always believed in me, and have given me the confidence to accompany them in various activities of their lives.

To my wife, **Pamela Konzi Epeke**, for the support she has always given me whenever I need it. The moments of silence that she imposes as a punishment when she chooses to manifest her whims have allowed me to devote myself to writing this book.

I can imagine the smile, the joy that will be on my parents' faces when they start reading this book.

To all my Subayi children, this book will serve as a substitute for your father whenever my absence is imposed on you.

I cannot remain indifferent to the people who appeared in my life like angels while I was going through a difficult time as a refugee in England,

Jeff and Allison Anderson, you're like an oasis in a desert to me. You had left an indelible mark on my family by your support that only angels of GOD can bring.

Colin and Kelcey Hill, you'll always be a family to us.

Frank and Esther Nseka, without you, my family would be a deluge. I am eternally in your debt.

Laland and Berny Mayall, as well as the whole Oldham ward, you had done your best so that I did not feel abandoned in England, words fail me to thank you.

Where the pain catches you is where you'll find your family. **The Ngoma family** in London, **the Tshulembo family** in Australia, **Lysette Kambu,** the big family of the **International Red Cross in** Manchester, as well as my fellow fighters from **RAS VOICE Refugee Actions,** thank you for giving me opportunities to smile while I was trying to rebuild my life.

A special thanks to **Mr. Willy Nonge**, for spending time reading the first part of the book and making some corrections.

Never forget that nature abhors emptiness.

SUMMARY

FOREWORD.

When you find yourself alone, after a death, a divorce, a relationship that has not gone well, or the loss of a job. When you feel this desire in you to rebuild yourself, take the time to read this book, it will be your friend.

This book will give you the paths to follow in order to rebuild yourself deeply. It will help you not to look back, but to hope for the best to come.

In this small book of personal development, the author compiles and recalls some of the teachings of great contemporary authors that allow man to rebuild himself.

To stop blaming each other all the time!

Not to put the blame on other people!

If you were able to love the other time, you can do it again. If you had been able to work and do well in your professional career in the past, you can do it again.

The power is in you! The abilities, the resources you need are buried deep within you. It is time to rebuild yourself, to be reborn.

"The 3 effective steps to rebuild your life" accompanies you to make peace with your past, to review some of your beliefs that probably didn't help in the past, also to identify what appetites you need to nourish in you to feel a complete man.

In one chapter of the book, you will be able to uncover the personality that is buried within you, the type of person you are, as well as that of the people around you. This discovery can help you pursue your professional career but also the same principles can be applied in family life.

If you have lost your job due to the behaviour of your boss or your colleagues, it is time to rebuild yourself. Stop blaming yourself and blame others.

"The 3 Effective Steps to Rebuilding Your Life" gives you clues to identify the kind of Boss who runs your business, how you can deal with the negativity of your boss and that of your colleagues.

I have worked a lot with young people in my profession and also in religious service. If you are still in this category of youth this book allows you to find your personal legend, your destiny and your mission.

This book challenges young people to do some deep introspection. Each young person will realize that they must decide as soon as possible whether they just want to be an **"addition to society" or they will have to be a "contribution to humanity"**.

Finally, **"The 3 Effective Steps to Rebuild Your Life"** gives you the tips to feed your appetites: **physical, spiritual, emotional, and intellectual appetites.**

In DR Congo, where I was born, when I was still in my twenties, I was exposed very early on to the roles of religious ministries as Bishop of a parish, then President of an archdiocese of more than three thousand families.

This priestly service has allowed me to accompany families, married couples, young boys and girls, single men and women, to solve their daily problems, to face their difficulties, and to organize all aspects of their lives.

For more than five years, I had managed to coach and transform the lives of tens of thousands of families by organizing self-help groups in several Central African countries through humanitarian, self-help, and employment programs that focused on how to make a business plan, improve family life, and solve problems in the community.

Later, I worked as a volunteer with the British Red Cross as a refugee counsellor and asylum seeker where I effectively helped several exiles with advice, guidance, and techniques to help them settle and better rebuild their lives in the host country.

At one point in my life, I found myself as an asylum seeker in England. During these moments of loneliness, time spent alone, away from my wife, children, friends, I decided to take on the project of writing this book to share my experience of how I managed to rebuild my own life.

"The 3 effective steps to rebuild one's life" is a synthesis of techniques drawn from my own experiences, from conferences, from the writings of other authors on personal development.

Introduction

Through this book, I do not pretend to set out new theories on personal development, or to evoke new subjects that could revolutionize the world.

This book is rather a compilation, a summary of important principles stated on personal development.

It seems that the world is becoming more and more a place where there is more despair, more problems, more challenges. More and more, since man has not had access from birth to instructions on how to use the real functions of his brain, on how his thoughts, personality, and behavior are formed, he is left to himself to face the realities of life.

We could, however, benefit from the advice of our parents, loving friends, educational systems, and sometimes the help of certain behavioural specialists such as psychologists, coaches, pastors, philosophers, etc.

It has been shown in England, where I am now, that the suicide rate is very high more than any other cause of death.

Stress, depression, loneliness make people kill themselves. So, it seems to some that taking one's life away is the easiest way to solve life's problems.

If you are considering being counted among those who kill themselves, ask yourself these questions first:

Do you want to be counted as a quitter? Who wants to be added to the list of losers? Will you want to be remembered as someone who didn't have enough strength to withstand the pressures of the world?

A Hungarian intellectual-philosopher, **Agnes Heller (1929-2019)** said :

Our age needs more than others a form of heroism that gives everyone the task of grasping what the present is all about. The task requires making oneself available for what is happening to us."

Living in these modern times requires **heroism and the willingness to face what is happening to us**, to **find solutions to our problems and not to let go**.

In the midst of these many modern difficulties and problems of life, we are blessed to inherit the writings of great thinkers, examples of the bravery of people who have lived through and overcome fear, terror, the problems of life, whether personal or collective.

Several centuries since mankind has existed, we have had a great legacy of men of bravery and courage who have been able to confront their fears and find solutions to problems that have arisen before them.

In writing these few words, I am thinking mainly of my children, and of the world we are leaving them.

I feel that no matter how many years I spend on earth, I probably won't have enough opportunity to tell them all I've learned about life. The multiple activities of life will still not allow me to have the opportunity to pass on all my individual experience to each of them so that they are morally armed, vaccinated against the difficulties they will encounter in their journey.

At least through these writings they can remember principles of tenacity that should characterize their lives. They will find a source of courage, dynamism, positive thoughts to rebuild their lives after mistakes they may make in their lives.

The world needs more and more courageous men to solve life's challenges. Families need fathers and mothers who do not shrink from challenges. Nations need Politicians who remain uncompromising, loyal to their ideologies, and who can give hope to peoples who are suffering. The countries of the world need statesmen who make promises and fulfil them.

In this book, as I say above, I simply had the desire to hammer on principles that build man and his mind.

This book expresses with all simplicity the theories that I believe are important for every human to finally take knowledge to forge his character, influence his environment, call for better circumstances in his favor.

The literary world has been blessed to know great thinkers, writers like **Vincent Norman Peal**, who has transformed the lives of thousands of people with his theories on positive thinking.

Humanity has been able to improve time management and performance at work thanks to the principle set out in the 80/20 theory advocated by the Italian **Vilfredo Pareto.**

And, most recently in modern life, the same theory has been further supported by the famous thinker, businessman, a free spirit man, the American **Timothy Ferris,** who in his book The **4-Hour Work Week** emphasizes the creation of a new class of men called the "New Blessed (NB)", men who do not kill themselves with long hours of work. Tim Ferris encourages men and women that they shouldn't reserve all the happiness for the end of their lives, when they retire, that might not happen, but rather he encourages them to live in the moment, take a mini retirement, and enjoy life while they work.

Stephen R. Covey, described **"The 7 Habits of Successful People"**, a jewel of principles, of truth, that truly transforms man's thinking towards success. **We will only be constructive as long as we start with the conclusion in mind. Know from the beginning where you want to** go," said **Steven R. Covey**.

On the other hand, in the face of the obstacles, battles, threats and wars that life offers, that nations make among themselves, it is important that every person living on earth has the opportunity to read and internalize the ideas of the Chinese Army General **Sun Tzu set** forth in his book, **"The Art of War",** an unparalleled classic.

When we're confused about not knowing how to define what life is. For those who cannot define their lives, they can give meaning to their lives by reading "**the game of life",** a cellular automaton imagined by **John Horton Conway**. They will actually discover if life is a game and not a fight.

Very late in my life, I met what I consider to be the great African scholar of the 20th century, **Professor CHEIKH ANTA DIOP**. His writings **in Negro Nations and Cultures**, **Civilization or Barbarity and others,** opened my eyes to reconsider my whole identity, the history of humanity, my spirituality and my future as an African. Professor **CHEICK ANTA DIOP** helped me to become aware of the deep alienation from which most African intellectuals suffer.

Professor **Cheick Anta Diop** has reframed the history of civilizations in the world. Anyone with a passion for good faith and intellectual objectivity should pay tribute to this scholar who has done great scientific work on the history of humanity and its civilizations.

Just to name a few, but there are many other authors who have inspired me and changed my mind.

These are generic books that I would like to be buried with to occupy my journey to the afterlife.

For an informed reader, having gone through several books on personal development, one would simply wonder if it is worth writing again, because almost everything has been said.

Indeed, it is in this perspective that this new book "**The 3 effective steps to rebuild one's life**" comes to remind humanity that much has been said and written to make us happy, to succeed in life, also to be in harmony with oneself and one's surroundings.

This book comes once again, hammering on positive thinking.

"**The 3 effective steps to rebuild your life**" in itself can take you on a journey of discovery of true principles of happiness that will boost your life forever.

This increasingly diverse world presents more opportunities but also more challenges. It is more than ever an imperative to sleep in your subconscious that attitude is more important than altitude. It's all about the mind first.

MAKE PEACE WITH ONE'S PAST.

Chap. 1 Making peace with one's past.

God cares much more about the person we are and the person we are going to become, than about the person we have been. He wants us to keep trying.

Dale R. Renlund.

Turn to yourself.

It is always easy to look at others, to see what they are doing, either to criticize or to encourage. But we spend less and less time looking at ourselves.

This reproach is made even in the Bible, for those who read it, ***Jesus of Nazareth asked this question:***

''Why do you see the straw in your brother's eye, and not see the beam in your eye?''. Matthew 7:3

If you look closely, you will see that man very often avoids spending time with himself. He avoids criticizing himself.

We spend a lot of energy to keep ourselves busy, to escape the gaze of our own person.

We struggle to be honest with others, but we make less effort to be honest with ourselves.

Whereas in order to make peace with our past, we must be able to take time, to observe ourselves, to talk to ourselves, to sit down with ourselves to sweep away what we no longer need.

It is still enough to observe well, one will discover that we are all in a hurry and always eager to meet the appointment with others, but very often we have difficulty meeting the appointment with ourselves. We run away from introspection. We flee from meditation. We flee from our consciousness. For the clever ones, they even manage to absorb substances such as drugs, alcohol, and others just to flee the encounter with oneself, with one's consciousness.

The invitation of this chapter is to turn to oneself. It is the first step towards inner peace.

Take time to look at ourselves, look at the best we are, the best we can be. To look at ourselves and see the complex being that we are, both holy and carnal, mixed with perfection and imperfection, desires to rise and at times threatened by feelings that bring us back down.

In the life of every human being, there will be a moment when we will not be able to go back, or we may realize that the harm that has been done cannot be undone.

The moment we feel that we have broken, through our past actions, an important relationship in our lives. Some memories of love turn to bitterness.

Even in the cupboard of our memories, we regret a mistake, a mistake made that cost us our work, that made our children's lives insecure.

Moreover, looking in the rear-view mirror of the past, we can realize that, if only we would have acted differently, the situation could have been saved or even not have come to this point.

In our past, we take with us people we wish we'd never meet, places we wish we'd never go even in our wildest dreams.

Man in his life cycle has behind him his past that will not fade, his present that he must live, and his future that he has to hope for.

From all that we could say about our past, once we take the time to respect the appointment with ourselves, we will find that all these events were for our own good. In every event of the past, good or bad, every person we meet, good or bad, there is always a lesson to be learned.

Our present, our future, depends on how we decide to deal with our past.

Our lives are changing, building on the lessons of the past. The past with its tears, its joys, its remorse, its consolations build our present, and strongly influence our future.

Here's a person who really needed to make peace with his past.

I had met a niece, who was 17 years old. I hadn't had a chance to see her grow up. It so happened that once we had made contact and got to know each other, we were soon spending a lot of time together talking to each other, just to make up for the time lost between niece and uncle.

Like most young people her age, the girl's conscience was charged with her first failed love experiences, which seemed to be characterized by some abuse. She felt out of place, lost her self-esteem, and gradually became withdrawn. Preferring to spend time in her room, either writing or sleeping. Pretty face, but lost her smile because she was totally trapped in her past that was eating away at her.

This is what she told me, in a few words:

"Uncle, I feel I no longer have any value as a woman. While we did not grow up in the same context with my mother, for her, a virtuous woman is one who kept her virginity until marriage. Several times I have tried to discuss this subject with my mother, but she seems not to be open-minded.

I don't care about my lost virginity, but rather about the abuse I experienced at the hands of this man whom I surrendered in first love when he was not honest.

He made a fool of me, treated me like dirt. And, he was just a simple profiteer. I feel dirty, without respect and dignity.

I would have liked to come back to my life a few years earlier to correct my mistakes but alas.

I'm locked in my room all the time. I prefer to either write in my diary or listen to my music rather than give myself up to someone. Whomever I can deliver my secret to, will listen to me with a judgement about me. Instead, I need to talk to someone who simply listens to me without passing judgment.

This girl was tormented from within. She was worried about things that could never come back.

More than anyone else, she needed to meet with herself. She needed to assess her wounds, her tears, her hopes. To take time with herself to draw strength to rebuild herself.

She couldn't keep running away.

Richard L. Evans made this observation:

"Sometimes and under certain conditions it is possible to escape from many things such as prison walls, false friends, bad company, boring people, old environments but never from ourselves. When we go to bed at night, we are there whether we like it or not. The most persistent thing in life (and, we

have no doubt, in death too) is our own self-awareness. That said, there is no more pitiful person than one who feels uncomfortable in his own company, no matter where he runs, how fast he runs or how far he runs". (Richards L. Evans, Book of Quotes from Richards L. Evans, Salt Lake city, Publisher Press, 1971, page 214).

The appointment with ourselves, with our own person brings us to the other steps to make peace with our past.

It is important that each person learns the necessary tools that pushes us to know what is running away inside us, what is happening inside ourselves, before going against it towards others.

It is indispensable to make from time to time his ***hygiene of conscience, to*** *clean his bottom, to make peace with oneself.*

We cannot sweep every day our room, our house, the outside of the plot, our town, our market, when inside ourselves we bury dirt inside us, when inside ourselves we have not been able to sweep.

''A pacified citizen, wakes up as a pacifying citizen'' *says* ***Thomas d'Ansembourg.***

Only when you have pacified yourselves, only when you have found peace in your consciousness, in your mind, can you stand up and go and build peace in your family, in your neighborhood, in your surroundings.

We cannot hope to contribute to the peace of others when we are not at peace with ourselves.

Men who have the strong ability to forgive others began first by forgiving themselves and finding inner peace within themselves. Then they had enough almost supernatural powers of surpassing themselves to forgive others.

The example of **Nelson Mandela and Gandhi** shows that they are people who have spent enough time with their own person, their own inner self, before they come out of prison and forgive their former torturers.

We cannot make peace with ourselves without taking these elements into account: **acceptance, control of our emotions over the past, finally making peace with ourselves**.

The Principle of Acceptance.

We cannot take a step forward without accepting each other.

The first thing to accept is that we cannot control everything.

We spend a lot of time and energy controlling ourselves, bringing ourselves back to order and striving to follow the established rules. Sometimes we do it well, but then we realize that we still fall back to where we came from.

"What I fear is what happens to me," exclaimed Job.

On the other side of this reality, we must recognize that we cannot control the actions of others.

Acceptance means acknowledging one's past, accepting it, knowing that no matter how much energy is expended to correct or bring back our past, it will never happen.

Just as the river of water does not flow back to its source, so our past would remain unchanged.

Does accepting your past mean agreeing with your past? Is accepting one's past the same as loving it? Or is accepting one's past tantamount to torturing oneself continually, perpetually, stirring the wound, dwelling on one's guilt?

The answer to these questions is "NO".

Accepting your past is just realizing it happened. That it happened, and there's nothing we can do to bring it back to where it started or even change it.

John Paul Sarte *said,* ***"We are all alive but some are dead, it is a living death to be surrounded by perpetual worries of judgements and actions that cannot be changed.***

We will be very disappointed if we continually try to dodge our past, to continually justify ourselves, it would be a great waste of energy.

There are pasts that will always hurt us no matter how hard we try to move forward. Either we were hurt or we were hurt. Maybe we had missed an opportunity we thought was unique that would have changed the course of our lives. We can continually brood over these memories day and night, but is that a solution?

Man has the power which is free will. We are free to change our negative emotions, our worries caused either by our own actions or by the actions of others. We can free ourselves from hell, from the shame that can be caused by the look or judgment of others.

Just as we can choose to change our attitude, to come out of the hell of worry and shame, just as if we stay there, we freely accept to live in hell.

Will you like to spend your whole life regretting and blaming yourself for this kind of situation year after year?

I know a young Arab girl who has always worried about the fact that she was deflowered before marriage, and is not sure how her parents will react after her wedding night when she gets married.

Another priest, a church leader, has long been hiding from the public. He had chosen to live with a girl from his choir with whom he had fallen in love and preferred to abandon his priesthood. He did not want to go outside for fear of facing the shame of his church members.

I also remember another young Cameroonian who was part of my self-governance group in a village in Cameroon. This young man's family had fallen into enormous precariousness but every day this young man would tell us his memories of Europe and the good life they had when their father was ambassador in the years before. This young man never stopped imagining and hoping only if that time could come back.

These people are somehow locked in the hell of the past.

I'm not saying that the past is unimportant or has no place in our lives.

But the place of the past is in what **Richard L. Evans** says. **He** stressed the importance of the past in everyone's life. He said in a speech at a conference in 1973 to an audience of thousands of people, the following:

''The past has its place, and is valuable for lessons learned. The present also has its place, and what we cannot change should not unnecessarily prevent us from looking and moving forward. Nothing lost or left behind should prevent us from becoming what we can become, from learning what we can now learn.

There are new decisions every day, every hour and reasons to improve and repent. Wherever we are, wherever we are, every day we have the opportunity to set the direction

Whatever the past, its meaning, its length, its losses, its lessons learned or left unlearned, we continue where we are wherever we are and become what we can become, with work, repentance, improvement, and with faith in the future''.

The only thing that we can change about our past is the perception, our attitude that we feel about these past events. *We can change our thoughts and emotions about our past.*

To detach ourselves from our emotions about our past.

The past brings with it emotions.

Emotions are buried in the man. They waver from day to day.

Man is a set of chemical composition. There are things that bubble inside us, sometimes they stay calm and then come out in a mood.

For an event that happened in our past, day after day, we can feel strong emotions in us, either joy, sadness, anger, or a mind that tears, or even our heart that palpitates very strongly.

It should be noted that there is nothing abnormal about feeling depressed, discouraged, sad or having negative feelings for a while as a result of certain past events.

These feelings happen to everyone. You don't have to feel guilty if you wake up one morning and you don't feel good.

All the great men we know have been depressed about one thing or another in their lives.

For Christians; there is no greater man than **Jesus Christ**. Christians believe in the divinity of Jesus Christ. They believe that he had supernatural power that was not of this world. But we still have to realize that despite this, he himself was depressed at one point in his life.

Matthew in the Gospels reports that Jesus Christ said this to his disciples:

My soul is sorrowful even unto death; abide here, watch with me'' Matthew 26:38

A Christian author, **Paul Calzada**, has made an excellent comment on this, saying :

This text of Scripture reassures us about the possibility for each one of us to experience moments of deep sadness. Jesus experienced a sadness so strong that it made him consider death, at that moment, as a way out. The temptation to die without the cross touched his mind for a moment.

This sadness is not a lack of faith, or even a sin.

Perhaps you have experienced, or know, such moments of deep sadness, letting you believe that death would be a way out! Don't blame yourself for feeling that way. Just as Christ experienced this time, it is normal that you too may go through such moments. Take courage in looking at Him. Consider that this sadness is not a lack of faith, or even a sin.

Unfortunately, for many believers, sadness and depression do not correspond to the image they have of walking in faith. They believe that a Christian should always be joyful, that he or she should be happy:

Remaining positive and strong in the face of adversity

Always do with joy all that needs to be done

Always be radiant

Remain at peace in all circumstances

It is rightly considered that a Christian can have a heart attack as a result of overwork, stress, fatigue... but, whether he (she) is sad and depressed, it is considered abnormal! Well, it is not! You may experience, after overwork, stress, fatigue, rejection... a deep sadness.

Admitting that sadness can get to you is already a step towards the possibility of getting out of it. Being in denial will never help you out of sadness. Denial puts you in even more anguish, especially if it is accompanied by the guilt generated by those who tell you that it is not normal to be sad.

Notice that not only does Jesus not deny his sadness, but he shares it with three of his closest disciples. (Matthew 26:38)

Do not deny your sadness, make it known to people you trust, ready to listen to you and to accompany you in prayer.

Well, these few lines of **Paul Calzada** apply to everyone, Christians, Muslims, atheists, Buddhists or non-believers, all of us can feel moments of great sadness. It is not important to feel guilty about it. It is a normal fact related to our essence as human beings.

Myself, I don't know how many times I have woken up with great feelings of sadness, sometimes with feelings of discouragement, great depression. Very often it's after misunderstandings, little arguments with my wife. My wife is the only person in the world who can plunge me into a state of great stress and depression, but she is also the only person in the world who knows how to bring me more joy than anyone else. I think this is the same for anyone who feels in love with another person.

What can we do to remain at peace in the face of hardship, in the face of these negative feelings?

The answer is to learn to detach oneself at all costs from the things that create these emotions.

Sarah Cavanagh, an English teacher, specialist in **Brahma Kumari** meditation, made this observation: "***When we detach ourselves into something, or someone, we also detach ourselves from the emotions that are connected to it".***

I fully agree with those who say that the opposite of love is not hate but indifference.

Indifference detaches us from the person, it detaches us from the emotions we feel for them.

In the same way we must detach ourselves from the past to detach ourselves from the emotions that are linked to it.

What you think is in line with your emotions, you cannot think badly of someone and feel love for them.

Each individual turns in a circle that influences him, that influences his life, his vision, his emotions, his moods.

Circle of influence. Emotions are created by what influences us on a daily basis, either good or bad.

Our circle of influence is made up of several things. It is everything we read, everything we look at, everything we hear every day will influence our emotions.

Social networks influence us enormously with more influencers, opinion leaders who can awaken or put to sleep our emotions, our old habits, our beliefs, our friends, the places we frequent.

That's how there are more and more influencers on social networks. We can find good ones that can elevate our emotions but unfortunately, most of these social network influencers, influence badly. Most social network influencers show another life in the media when in reality they are quite different.

The advent of social networks has given voice and credit to people who, in real life, do not even deserve the attention and scrutiny of the public.

As the Italian writer **UMBERTO ECCO (1932-2016) put it** so well, ***social networks have given voice to legions of fools who used to talk only in the bar and did no harm to the community. They were silenced at once. Today they have the same right to speak as a Nobel Prize winner.***

Among these privileged fools, mentioned by **Umberto ECCO,** are pseudo-pastors, pseudo-journalists and improvised columnists, pseudo-musicians with no educational content in their works.

Also, among the misdeeds of social networks, a large part is made up of publications that demonstrate the opposite of reality in the lives of these people.

We see pictures of people dressed well, drinking, eating their fill when in reality they live in immense poverty.

We see couples posting videos and photos as if they were living in perfect harmony, whereas in their real life it's a disaster.

People who give the impression that they spend their days at the office, while they are unemployed.

Arthur C. Brooks, president of the American Enterprise Institute, saw clearly how people use and consume social networks, he said it this way at a conference in Salt Lake city :

When we use social media, we tend to broadcast the smiling details of our lives, but not the hard times at school or at work. We describe an incomplete, sometimes false life.

We share this life, and then we consume the almost exclusively false lives of our social media friends.

Then he asks this question:

How could you spend part of your time pretending to be happier than you are, and the other part of your time seeing how much happier others seem to be than you are?

Many spend all their days in social networks and find themselves influenced by false lives, their own false lives and those of their follower friends.

Note, everything you see, read and listen to daily is part of your circle of influence.

To detach ourselves from the emotions of the past, we must ask ourselves the question:

Does what I read, what I look at, what I see, what I hear give me peace? Doesn't it send me back to the emotions of past events?

Thus, the person who really wants to detach himself from the emotions of the past that do not produce peace will have to scan his thoughts daily, as well as all the elements that influence him.

There are photos we won't need to look at anymore to make peace with our past. Things we don't want to read anymore, lyrics, songs we don't want to hear anymore, words and names we don't even want to say anymore just to get rid of and make peace with our past.

The daily management of our circle of *influence is very necessary if we want to move forward and leave the past behind us.*

Negative emotions, a drop in motivation brings us down.

So, even if we cannot change our past, but at least we must control, change the emotions we feel about the events of the past so that we have to make peace with ourselves.

If we don't control our thoughts well it will influence our body, our behaviour and even the circumstances that will happen to us in the future.

Finally, being at peace with yourself.

Once you've made an appointment with yourself. We had time to listen to each other. Then had the courage to accept our past. It's time to make peace with yourself.

To be wrong in one way or another is simply a representation of a certain mental disharmony that we ourselves have experienced.

Appreciating oneself is the vital element for making peace within oneself.

Once I attended a personal development conference, the speaker encouraged a technique to actually appreciate oneself. He said that in order to accept and appreciate ourselves as we are, we have to find three or five things around us every day that we have to be grateful for.

Very often we take everything we have for granted until it is taken away from us or disappears.

We will greatly appreciate the blessing of having eyes that see when we can take time to simply enjoy the sunrise, the beauty of the flowers that surround us, the beauty of mountain scenery, built cities, the immensity of rivers, streams, lakes, sea.

We can simply find time to listen to bird music in the morning to enjoy the blessing of having ears that listen.

Each person can find three or five things that can help him or her appreciate who he or she is on a daily basis. Parents who are always there for their children, a faithful friend who always gives his ears to listen to the other person's grievances. Are we grateful for teachers who take time to transform our lives, to forge our personalities?

Very often we later earn a better living than those teachers who taught us to read and write. But sometimes we simply forget to be grateful that they came into our lives.

Even when we are in an unsuitable situation, even in a hospital bed, we can always find three or five things that we can appreciate from the fact that we are still alive.

Never blame others for what happens to us. Just as we have had time to emphasize that we should not dwell on condemning ourselves perpetually for our past actions, so too we should not always point the finger at others for our mistakes, or simply for what happens to us.

Do not be among those who misunderstood Jean Paul Sartre by saying: *"Hell is the other" in his play "Huis clos".*

We can't always blame others for what happens to us. A man only becomes a man when he stops complaining and blaming others as the author of his own misfortunes, when he stops complaining about circumstances that present themselves to his disadvantage, but rather he becomes a man when he knows how to make his defeats profitable, and begins to use these harmful circumstances as an aid to his progress.

There are times when the direction of your life will depend on the decision that others will have to make about you. Whatever the outcome of their decision, have the courage to rub your hands together and move on. Don't blame others for our own mistakes, because they are in a position to decide on your life. Take it upon yourself, and learn from it.

Once again, my life as a refugee has taught me that lesson. For a moment, I found myself faced with the reality that the direction of my life no longer depended on me. My life to get back on track again, to get a job, to continue to study as I wanted, to move around as I wanted, depended on the decision that immigration officers had to make. It depended on my wife who had to decide whether or not she wanted to do family reunification to join them in the U.S. where she had already found asylum. So whatever I could do, it was up to them to decide my fate.

When decisions on both sides dragged on. One Sunday morning before going to church, I wrote these words in my diary:

''You, *the people watching me, surely you'll ask me how I am?*

I will always tell you that I am fine, even when yesterday night my pillows were wet with my tears, I am always fine.

I'm fine would still be my answer to that generic question.

Like a soldier forging his mind in difficult exercises, like me, I will find my joy and answers in the difficult things in life.

You're probably going to ask me how I feel right now? I'll tell you that I feel like I'm in the middle of the sea.

I don't know how to go back where I came from or forward where I'm going.

From where I'm standing, I can see a rescue boat that can get me back safely. But alas, it depends on the disposition of the heart of the captain of this famous rescue boat.

If he has a sense of humanity, he could come to my rescue, otherwise I would be left to my own fate.

At this very moment, my life no longer depends on myself.

In the meantime, I have to swim. Swim with all my strength, swim even when I haven't learned to. I'm swimming in a despair that can bring life back to life.

What does this trawler do? Does it see me moving? Will it be able to send me the lifebuoy?

He's the only one with the answer.

Maybe right now the interest in keeping the border secure outweighs my life.

Maybe he sees me coming, but he'd rather see me die because my life might interfere with his.

I'm in the middle of the sea, swimming, not knowing how to go back and forth.

This lifeboat I see in the distance is full of immigration officers who have to decide my fate.

I see that they are still thinking, debating whether they should preserve their country's migration policy or save the life of a stranger they do not know.

I also see across the side, far away in this boat, the person holding this Lifebuoy is my wife. She, who has already had asylum and can save me.

But I wonder why she's dragging the buoy towards me, is she still the same person after all these years of separation?

Doesn't she consider whether my life would interfere with her new life built on her land of asylum?

I rub my eyes to make sure I can still see. Well, I confirm that I'm not blind, I'm not hallucinating either, she's the one who has the lifeline in her hand!

In the meantime, I've decided to swim. I have no choice but to swim.

Swimming among the sharks, among the whales. Swimming against my will.

Swinging my hands and legs around is the only thing I have to do.

I seem to still see that lifeboat. There it is. I can still hope.

The commander, the immigration officers, my partner, seems to be deciding my fate again.

Those who asked me in the beginning if I was all right, are still asking questions among themselves. This time they are wondering what brought him to the middle of the sea. Didn't he have another solution? Has he thought it through enough to get to that point? Why did he take such a risk?

Unfortunately, I don't know how to answer that. Once I open my mouth, I'll take a sip of water and risk drowning.

Let me swim. Time will answer you in the end. Time has the answer to everything.

Oldham, Manchester, Sunday, 15 September 2019

Sometimes the decision of our lives would be in other people's hands, let's not blame them for that. We simply have the choice to continue swimming in deep water without opening our mouths too much.

We still don't need to know how it all ends. Sometimes it's important to take things as they come, step by step.

A Martin Luther King painting I always had in my refugee room said this:

''You still don't need to see the whole staircase, just decide to take the first step''.

When faced with certain circumstances, just take the first step, other things will follow of their own accord.

We'll have to make peace within ourselves. What are the feelings that go through you right now when you think about this or that person? Is it always animosity? Is it the spirit of revenge? Or is it even the desire to see him or her disappear? If there is always this feeling in a person's soul, it shows that this individual has not yet found peace in himself.

Spending time alone can bring us peace. There are enough noises around us that prevent us from finding deep peace. Sometimes we have to censor ourselves from using technology for one, two days in order to find serenity. Days away from the phone, without emails, without technology can bring us peace.

The moment of solitude allows us to ask ourselves real questions that allow us to know what we are, and what we would like to be in the future.

It is in the quiet, peaceful moment that we ask ourselves, who am I? What would I like to be at this moment? What would I like to be in the future?

Would I prefer to remain what I am now? Or what I was five years ago? Or would I like to become another person in the future years?

Solitude is used to determine the direction to follow.

In this modern world, where people are constantly busy with the internet, social networks, smart phones, those who succeed are those who know how to concentrate. Successful people are those who manage to make the sacrifice of staying a little isolated and thinking.

Covid-19: An opportunity to isolate yourself.

As I am writing this book, like most people in the world, I have been confined to my house for almost two months now, in solitude and isolation.

The 2019 Corona Virus Decease has successfully confined more than 3.38 billion people worldwide. This figure was given by the French online newspaper "**LA LIBERATION**" published on March 31, 2020, at 12:19.

This disease has claimed more lives than one would imagine. There is no doubt that after this confinement step, when everything will be back in order, the COVID-19 has already proven itself enough for its logo resembling antennas, to be placed in museums around the world so that the people could remember the damage caused by this pandemic. We regret the death of our close relatives, friends, famous people who died from this disease. The global economy of almost every country has been affected. The world kneeling, observes with uncertainty how scientists, doctors, laboratory workers are fighting to find the cure or a vaccine that will eradicate this pandemic.

Even the solidarity that exists between people who have been touched by COVID-19. We had seen scenes where the Chinese were threatened by certain rascals on the buses, the subways just because the virus appeared at their home in the city of Wuhan (Hubei). Likewise in China, there has been a scene of isolated violence, of discrimination against certain minority communities, black in particular, accused of not respecting the containment measures and could be at the basis of the spread of the virus.

Beyond all of the aforementioned harms of this pandemic, containment imposed to reduce the spread of the disease brings with it the opportunities for the 3.38 billion people confined to their homes around the world.

The confinement has given billions of people the opportunity to meet up with themselves in isolation. There is no better opportunity like this for everyone to isolate themselves, to do deep introspection, for personal meditation.

No doubt it is that after this global confinement life would be much better for those who will survive than before. Those who stay alive will have learned good habits of handwashing hygiene, consumption, saving a good time.

The people who will survive this pandemic will learn from this experience that it will now be necessary to leave your home only when necessity requires it. With this attitude, there would be less pollution, less unnecessary traffic jams in the main arteries.

After confinement, those who will have made the most of the solitude, who will respond to the meeting with their own person, will manage to improve the quality of their life, of the life of their family, since there will be a large number of divorce among couples whose relationship has become toxic. Confinement would help them look face to face for several days to deal with their problems. Likewise, there will also be a large number of couples and families who will come out much more fulfilled at the end of confinement, because they will have to take advantage of this time to have a good time together. There will be parents who will get to know their children much better, children who will again enjoy the company of their parents, siblings, and learn more about their family history. Another good thing about this confinement, we will learn to appreciate certain things that we take for granted. Love, solidarity, sharing will increase in the hearts of men because we realize that we have all fought and defeated a single common enemy. In the neighborhoods, the neighbors will appreciate the presence of each other because they missed each other during confinement.

We see that even in the worst moment, we can still have hope. Where men fail, nature itself can take care of it.

I am very impatient to live this life which promises to be a very good life after confinement. I can't wait to hug my wife again, go for a walk and play with my children, enjoy the smile of my colleagues, friends without fear of being infected. We will all learn that nothing is for granted, we live by grace each time we wake up in good health, we can run without getting tired, we breathe without the help of a respirator, walk and wander around big cities without being afraid to respect the social distance of one meter.

I firmly believe that beyond crying than leaving this pandemic, life would be much better again if only the 3.38 billion confined people took advantage of this isolation to make peace with themselves. Even, as well as with his entourage.

To summarize this chapter, we say that what you think translates into your emotions, later it is translated into action.

You can't think badly of someone and feel love for them.

To get out of the slavery of our past, whether it is a better past that we would like wholeheartedly to see happen again, or a smelly past that stinks, we are simply called to get rid of it.

The future is better, our gaze should be forever fixed forward, towards the future where we will spend the rest of our lives. The future always holds some very beautiful episodes in store for us.

There are no stronger words than Isaiah's words in the Bible to summarize this chapter and make peace with his past:

Don't think about past events,

And no longer consider what is old.

Here, I'm going to do something new that's about to happen:

...I'll put a path in the desert,

And rivers in solitude. (Try 43: 18-19)

Let us summarize some of the principles set out in this chapter:

1. Turning to oneself is the first step in making peace with one's past.
2. ***Solitude is used to determine the direction to follow***
3. *Just as the river of water does not flow back to its source, so our past will remain unchanged. So we must accept this.*

4. *Our present, our future, depends on how we decide to deal with our past.*
5. *When we detach ourselves from something or someone, we also detach ourselves from the emotions associated with it. Thus, we must detach ourselves from the past in order to detach ourselves from the emotions associated with it.*
6. The daily management of our circle of influence is very necessary if we want to move forward and leave the past behind us.
7. Sometimes the decision of our life would be in other people's hands, let's not blame them for that.

Chap. 2. When it burns, always go out the fire escape.

"The true greatness of a man is measured when all goes wrong.

Martin Luther King.

When I was an asylum seeker in England with a rigorous immigration system, faced with people who gave the impression that they were trained only to not believe everything that asylum seekers would tell them.

For two years I was refused on my application, separated from my family, worried about my children who were still small and wanted their father by their side.

Faced with this situation, the tendency is to stay in bed and not move, as many asylum seekers do. It felt like isolation.

Very often we were deeply depressed. We used to complain about the slow immigration system. Sometimes we were demoralized because we were in a situation that was not up to us, and we didn't know when it would end.

But as the days went by, I realized that no matter what my concerns, I would not force the immigration officers to give me the protection I was asking for.

Often between two appointments, it takes more than five months to go to the judge, an immigration officer.

To resolve this situation, I decided to make positive use of these waiting times for a final decision on my asylum application, which were spread over time. While I was in a waiting period to make appeals and appeals, I decided to maximize my time by doing online training, one of these training courses chosen was to do my Project Management training, pass my certification, also Human Resources training.

Later, immigration refused me again and declared me an "AER" (Appeal Right Exhausted). With this status, I no longer had the right to appeal, but I had the possibility to introduce other evidence, a new asylum application, in other words, to start the whole procedure all over again from scratch. They gave me another six months to wait just for another appointment.

Positively I decided not to complain about my fate, the idea came to me to occupy my time writing this book, and also to improve my English.

I left England with more certificates and professional training, with the manuscript of my book, A Diploma in Project Management Program (PMP), certificates in Human Resources, Math, and English.

I was having a wonderful time helping other refugee claimants, helping them to present their cases properly. I got to know some wonderful people who taught me a lot about teamwork whether it was for the **International Red Cross** or in the campaign groups called **RAS VOICE of** England.

I don't think I would have had much more free time in my life like that period. Although it was accompanied by a lot of frustration, in the end it produced positive results in terms of personal progress.

This example is not so special, there are those who have had to do better than me in the same situation, but quite simply, I would like to illustrate that even in our worst bad times, there are positive things we can take advantage of.

Your circumstances may not be great, but they won't stay worst forever.

There will always be times when we will be faced with serious problems, serious difficulties in life. Moments when we have the impression that the sky is dark, the night becomes very long. Moments that we have been waiting impatiently for the cock to crow so that morning will finally come. Sometimes we don't even want the morning to arrive because it would bring with it tons of problems to solve.

I felt that moment the night I had to sign my letter of resignation in a job I liked. I thought about the colleagues I had to leave, the staff, the people I served. That night seemed to be endless.

I had a long night the day I was denied a visa for the fourth time to visit my children in the USA when I had a baby who was already 3 years old whom I had not yet seen, and three other small children who had not seen their father for several years. I had tears all night and thought about when I will see my children again.

The night was more painful when I learned of the death of my loved ones. An uncle, a nephew, two of the friends who had become like brothers to me. One was my best man, and the other had died when 2 days before he was well, he had even invited me to a restaurant that night. We each ate our favorite food, but alas, two days later I got a phone call that he was dead.

These were moments of great bitterness during which I had the impression that this shock would remain forever in my heart.

You may find yourself in a very difficult period of your life, but the good news is that any period is fleeting. There's nothing that remains status quo.

The good news is that no matter what we are going through, 100 years from now none of us currently living on earth would still be alive. All our problems will pass with us. So there's no point in us getting upset.

If you perceive an ideal, try to reach it. Aim for the moon, or else you'll reach for the stars.

The golden rule is that you should always try to get out through the emergency door even when the house is burning down.

A calm mind brings with it the solutions to any problem. A cool head solves everything.

It's easy to get carried away, to shout, to try to index others, but when we stay calm, our mind will give us all the resources we need to solve the dilemma and equation before us.

The Boxer Theory.

I like boxing matches. I don't like the violence of this fight but rather the lessons I learned from another point of view.

Beyond the health benefits, sociology, boxing teaches us several things.

Nelson Mandela made this observation:

''I didn't enjoy the violence of boxing as much as I enjoyed the silence. I was intrigued by the way you moved your body to protect yourself, how you used a strategy to catch and retreat, how you fought for a match.

Boxing is egalitarian, in the ring, rank, age, colour and wealth are unimportant. I never really fought after entering politics. My personal interest was training. I found rigorous exercise an excellent outlet for tension and stress. After intense training, I felt both mentally and physically lighter.

It was a way of losing myself in something that wasn't wrestling. After the evening training, I would wake up the next morning feeling strong and rested, ready to resume fighting" (Mandela, Long work to freedom.)

For any informed observer watching a boxing match, there are many things that he can learn that he can put into practice in his daily life.

Just like Mandela, the way a boxer protects his body, attacks his opponent, rests between rounds, retreats, has seriously inspired me in my daily life. I understood that there are imperatives in life that I must protect. I knew that I would not survive in certain circumstances without putting strategies in place to rebuild my life.

All of these lessons, I call it **the boxer theory**.

Lesson one: Protect your skull.

We can learn from boxers that the most important job to do in a fight is to protect your skull.

First of all, he is of the opinion of all sportsmen and women that a good boxer is the one who knows how to give punches and also how to take them. In the same way, in the fight of life you have to know how to give punches and also learn at certain times to accept them.

But, the most important thing in a boxer is to protect his head, his skull.

Well, protect your brain when the problems torment you.

Life gives us blows. We can receive blows from everywhere. It could come from work, it could come from our health, it could come from friends, family, or even love can disappoint us.

The blows of life can come even where we least expect it, such as in our own family, in places like churches, where we think we are a safe place, a place that is made up of people who should be living the higher law of love but where we can find ourselves around people who judge us by the measure that they themselves will not want to be judged.

Another milieu is the world of politics. It's the world of cheap shots par excellence.

We must be prepared for all of this, as a famous American Christian prophet, **Thomas S. Monson** observed:

Life is full of difficulties, small ones and bigger ones. It seems that there is an infinite supply of trials for each of us...Sometimes it seems that we don't see the end of the tunnel, that we don't see a dawn to break the darkness of the night. We feel the pain of broken hearts, the disappointment of dreams shattered and the desperation of vanished hopes...

We feel abandoned, overwhelmed with grief, alone... we may ask ourselves: Is there no balm in Gilead? (Finding Joy on the Journey, 2008).

There will be no shortage of blows in the path of life. But most importantly, protect your skull.

Please protect your skull. Please don't let the blows of life reach your nervous system.

Always let your head cool down. Don't act hot. A good motor always gives a good output.

Don't let life's difficult situations reach your brain, your head. Don't let it destroy your reasoning mechanism, destroy your nervous system. The head is the center of everything.

Vincent Paul Norman pointed this out so well that the only function of the whole body is to support the brain. This is where any solution comes from.

Protect your brain, please protect your skull.

Lesson two: Take a rest between rounds.

Another piece of wisdom to be drawn in a boxing match is the rest one takes after the bell rings. This moment in a boxing match allows the boxer to go and recharge with his coach.

So for a man, it's important in between rounds to sit down, listen to the coach, get your strength back, and then get back on the field.

The coach can be your parents, a close friend willing to listen to you, your love. He can be a teacher, a coach, or even an inspirational book. The main thing is to stop the fight and sit down before resuming another round.

Between two difficult situations, sometimes silence is golden. In front of people's criticisms, in front of rumours, false accusations on both sides. The right answer is to remain calm, silent, say nothing. Remain authentic in yourself.

Keep your cool, keep quiet. Time heals everything.

What you need to know. While we ourselves are suffering from the nightly pain of a tooth infected with decay, or even an abscess that is dragging on dying, in this moment of suffering, we are very indifferent to the number of thousands of deaths around the world. Even if we were told that there is a severe famine in a village in Brazil, or that Ebola disease is still surfacing in the east of the DR Congo and causing thousands of deaths, or even that the television stations are looping the devastation caused by the war in part of Syria, none of these problems will be more important to us than our own abscess which is due to burst that night.

In some situations only time heals, only hope, silence and patience remain the only watchwords. Know that despite your cries and complaints, there is a greater chance that the world will remain indifferent.

Doesn't the death of the eminent and famous of the world teach us?

No matter where you are under the sun, everyone is entitled to one minute's silence in memory of our death.

Living men do it because they care about their time. They are concerned about their own commitments.

Have you ever learned that life stopped because a great man of the earth died?

Then nothing will stop because you're not well, not even your death will stop things.

Instead of complaining about your problems, keep silent, only time solves everything.

Your problems will never be more important than the harm caused by the tooth decay of the person you are going to ask for help.

While you're taking a step back. Do what **Sun Tzu**, in his book "The **Art of War,"** advises, he says:

"Five main things must be the object of our continual meditation and care.... Use what you see, hear, and do not neglect to acquire new knowledge and all the help that can lead us happily to a good end.....

These five elements are: doctrine, time, space, command, discipline.

Lesson three: Have a doctrine.

Capture a thought to help you through your difficult times. Hold on to an ideology, a positive thought, a positive slogan that will give you a boost every time you are in your bad days.

Since I was 17 years old, positive thoughts, positive words from the great writer Paul Norman Vincent, have always helped me to overcome the trials and difficult episodes of my life. I use them every time I am faced with a difficult situation.

For example, the adage: **"Every disadvantage is an advantage"** has always been my motto even when I was unemployed for a long time. These 6 words pushed me to see the positive side of unemployment and took advantage of this disadvantage to do more vocational training, more community service, more voluntary service in organizations, also to rest and listen to the music I like. So, I have experienced what I can call ***profitable unemployment***. *Remember, every disadvantage is an advantage.*

When I resigned in 2017 as Regional Manager for Central Africa, an influential position in a very influential organization in the region. The thought of the Holy Scriptures accompanied me in rebuilding myself: ***When one door closes, seven other doors open...*** This word was always in my mind until I rebuilt myself and found other openings for my professional career.

Have a doctrine, hold a positive thought in your hand, in your time of retreat.

When the bell has rung for you to step back, you rest and listen to your coach's advice and then get back in the ring, let your mind cling to an ideology, a teaching, a thought, a name that can boost you.

Whether you are an atheist or a believer, Christian or Muslim, enter a name that will give you a boost. Either a name of divinity that can give you strength, or a name of one of your ancestors who was valiant, it does not matter, but stick to a name, a thought, a doctrine that will encourage you. Recite it from time to time, meditate on it, find your own way to remember it.

Musicians, movie actors, sportsmen and women know better than anyone else.

Each time an album is released, he gives himself a new name. For example, Koffi Olomide, a Congolese musician, understood this well. Sometimes he was called **Rambo** at one point, *later* **Papa Bonheur**, **Quadra Koraman**. He even takes the names of other famous people to enhance himself, *Sarkozy, Mr Donald Trumps, etc.*. These names and other slogans are self-motivating for these musicians.

When things go wrong, hold on to an ideology, a thought, even a name that will remind you of a triumph.

Lesson Four: If you have to, make others think you are asleep.

I don't know how many times in my life I spent more than six months, nine months deciding not to share my phone number with people around me. More than once, I deactivated my Facebook account, my Instagram, to retreat. I often do it to finally fake my sleep, to fake my death.

Pretend sometimes to be weak so that your enemies, opening the door to presumption and pride, come or attack you and let themselves be caught in a trap carved for them. Pretend to die if you must, you will discover those who are really with you," hammered the Master of War, ***Sun Tzu.***

Benefit, with every withdrawal I make, I manage to find out who is really, a friend, a brother, a real colleague on whom I can rely, and also I always manage to unearth the fakes of the true of what has surrounded me.

Lesson five: Don't let the sounds of spectators bother you.

As in a boxing match, don't be intimidated or distracted by the shouts and songs of the spectators.

Whether you've been kicked or are being kicked right now, you'll always be listening in the back of the room to people screaming.

During the fight of the century between **Mohammad Ali and George Foreman**, in 1974 people chanted this song for Ali:

''Ali Boma ye, Ali Boma ye, Ali Bomaye, Ali boma ye...

He was shouting in Lingala, a beautiful African language, these words translated into French meaning simply Ali kills him, Ali kills him....

(Shouts of spectators in the 1974 Zaire fight between Mohamed Ali and George Foreman).

That scream might have thrown George Foreman off balance. He even lost that fight to the great Ali.

Reflecting at length on the stage, I see that in real life, we will always hear cries of either encouragement or discouragement around us.

There will always be people who will criticize you, whether you did well or not. Mockers will always exist.

Do we have to pay attention to people's criticisms, mockery, judgments?

Note, don't let these spectator songs make you lose control. The boxer in the ring must not pay attention to insults, shouting, throwing insults at him. He should keep his eye on his opponent.

Attach yourself to your mission, keep your eye on your objectives, continue to fulfil your task, remain vigilant, and above all remain attached to your principles.

Nothing a man says will be able to change the opinion of what others think of him. If a third person wants to keep an opinion, a version of facts about you, let them speak and remain authentic.

At one point in his life, **Socrates the philosopher was** facing a lot of criticism, in front of his trial against the crowd that accused him, he quoted these words:

''The accusers in the shadows I can't see, I can't answer!''

Never respond to people, to the crowd you can't see. It would just be a waste of time.

Too often we worry too much about things even that are not as we think they are.

We don't protect our heads by indulging in worrying about others' judgments about us.

The brain can be overheated and tormented because of things that are said about us, or that are said to us directly or indirectly.

Sometimes when we regret that a person doesn't behave the way we would like them to behave but they do the opposite, we get into a general state of alert, worry, get angry, and overheat our minds.

And yet **Sadguru**'s wisdom says, ***if you want to make yourself unhappy, the opportunities are endless, because there will always be someone who will do something you don't like.***

Worse still, many times we allow ourselves to be disturbed by things that are less important, things that do not have enough impact on us. We allow them to disturb our sleep, to make our heart throb, and to torment us to the point of destroying our way of thinking.

There's a newspaper article that appeared in 1989 in the United States that states:

One day, a man who had been slandered by a newspaper went to Edward Everett to ask him what to do. Everett told him, "Do nothing!'

Half the people who bought the paper didn't see the article. Half the people who saw it didn't read it. Half of those who did read it, didn't understand it. Half of those who did understand it, did not believe it. Half of those who believed it, didn't care anyway'.

(Sunny Side of the Streets, November 1989, voir Zig Ziglar, stay up, up, up in a down, down Word 2001, p.174)

This man was overheating his head, his skull for imaginary things that perhaps don't exist in the way he imagined.

Sometimes you just have to step back. Stay quiet. Don't do anything!

Just like in a boxing match, take a step back. Take a seat. Listen to coach. Learn from what happened.

By staying calm in your corner, with a calm and cool mind, you have to combine these 3 ingredients to solve all problems:

Knowledge, reflection and faith.

It is time to summarize the principles set out in this chapter:

1. A calm mind brings with it the solutions to any problem. A cool head solves everything.
2. There will be no shortage of blows in the path of life. But most importantly, protect your skull.
3. Between two difficult situations, sometimes silence is golden. In the face of people's criticism, rumours, false accusations on both sides. The right answer is to remain calm, silent and authentic within oneself.
4. *When everything goes wrong, hold on to an ideology, a thought, even a name that will remind you of a triumph, it will be a source of motivation.*
5. Too often we worry too much about even things that are not as we think they are.

Chap. 3. Lemon is only important when it has juice.

"Every man values himself,
The price we are worth ourselves is given to us by others,
"And man is made great or small by his own free will.
Johann Von Schiller.

Principle of juice and lemon.

We have to remember that in this world we live in, "Lemon is only important when it has juice."

Sometimes it is hard to realize with bitterness that you will only be important if you have something important in your hands.

The world will look upon you with respect. It will consider you if you hold a good position in society, if you have a bank account, a good social position. You will be more valuable if you even have a reputation in the community.
I have to go so far as to say that we can even manage to respect you just because of your muscles, your biceps.

This is how it is disappointing at times to see that the one who was considered a strong man, deprived of his possessions, falls very ill because he finds that his entourage does not give him the same respect he used to have.

This world is a meeting place of giving and receiving.

Society is so materialistic that we can note with disappointment that you will be judged by what you bring, and when you are not able to do so, your name will disappear.

In sports. This truth is deeper, more alive in the world of sports.

The world's greatest athletes, top-level athletes, whom the world has celebrated for years, but just because of poor physical condition due to an inability to perform as they should, the world has put them in oblivion.

There are many examples in history of people who have been put in the dungeons just because they ran out of juice.

For several years the world has known Michael Schumacher (born January 3, 1969), a German driver, world champion in car racing, he is the only one in the world to have won seven successive times the Formula 1. In 2005, he was quoted in the Forbes store as the 2nd highest paid sportsman in the world. Schumacher broke records for years and years. The world revered Michael Schumacher with many exploits, until 2012 when he won his last Brazilian Grand Prix.

Everything was going well until December 29, 2013 when the world collapsed on this great Formula 1 racing star. While he was skiing in the Alps with his 14-year-old child. He had a fatal accident, his head hit a big rock. He was quickly evacuated by helicopter to France. Michael Schumacher broke his legs, his shoulder and then he was put in a coma for several months to undergo brain surgery. He was already retired, but that was the end of the name in the media, the company.

From that time until this day, nobody talks about him. In the beginning some people would go to the hospital to lay wreaths of flowers, but then nothing. Announced from time to time between his house and the hospital, his name is no longer mentioned. It's as if nothing exists about him. The great Formula One hero, Michael Schumacher, is out of juice.

It's just an illustration of a person who in his lifetime, rain or shine, the world must have always remembered him. There are a lot of famous people like him in this kind of situation.

All of this teaches that we only matter when we are able to bring something extra, an added value in the microcosm of society.

Lemon only matters when it has juice!

In love and friendship. The constant is a little bitter. We know many couples who are in very good health, in full bloom, very often it is because of either the woman's or the man's finances which are still stable. Either the health of the man or the woman still responds perfectly. Either, one partner in the couple is attracted by the social position of the other, or perhaps by the physical appearance, the intellectual capacity or simply just to bear the name of the man. Where do these beautiful prophetic words of Isaiah come from?

And seven women shall take hold of one man in that day and say: We will eat of our bread, and we will clothe ourselves with our garments, only let us be called by ***thy name... Isaiah 4:1***

The fact is that we are never loved for nothing! We are loved for the juice we have in our lemon. We are accepted for what we are, for what we have, or for what we bring, or finally for what we can bring.

Lemon only matters if it has juice!

What happens when the lemon loses its juice? When salt loses its flavour?

For example, statistics show that when it comes to finances, most couples have difficulty communicating. Financial management is at the root of many disputes and divorces.

"Good account makes good lovers," they say.

The same can be said about physical condition, a good professional position, a good place in society, that once you leave, you can leave friends, lovers, lovers, certain family members who were around.

I lived a similar story on the Ivory Coast when I was only 19 years old as a missionary. I went on a religious mission in Abidjan. While we were proselytizing with another American missionary. We became part of a family of 4 children, a husband and a wife.

Directly, I noticed the inadequacy, the imbalance that there was in the head of command in the couple. The woman was talking a little too much. She was very fat, giving orders to the man.
Either he had to wash this or that child, or clean up this or that thing.

The woman had to go to work so that the man could take it out on us. Once, it was just the three of us with the man. He made us pull out a picture, an old picture from 3 years ago. You could see how he had flesh on his skin. He was very cute in the picture. He seemed to breathe life.

He looked at these photos with admiration, he told us about his old job, how he lost it. He told us about how little by little the woman had to go out to get the money and he had to take care of the children. Little by little, temptation took its place, distance was created, love diminished. Little by little the man lost his authority. The couple began to put up with the fact that in the name of the children, he did not know how to make an extreme decision. He wanted to keep his family together, but at what price? More and more the man felt very bad.

We are not saying that all women will act the same. This is a frequent case, the man or the woman can find themselves diminished, no longer considered just because what used to be their couple no longer exists. Quite simply, the lemon only mattered when there was juice.

Suddenly, tears ran down his cheeks and he finally uttered a word that would be engraved in my memory for years to come. He said: "Dear friends, pray for me, pray also for yourselves, so that whatever the situation, that God may spare you from becoming dependent on one person (my wife in my case), you will lose a lot of your esteem.... Then he concluded by adding this: lemon has value only when there is juice".

I don't know how true those words are in real life. Certainly, everyone finds himself in different situations, but at least one thing in common, dependence weakens man.

Since then, in my daily prayer, this sentence has not been missing: "MY GOD SAVES ME FROM THE SITUATION WHERE I WILL BE TOTALLY DEPENDENT ON SOMEONE".

I observed the same situation with a friend, who was very stable for several years. Married, father of a family, with a good job for many years, the water was flowing under the bridge in peace. Life seemed to be smiling at him. But suddenly, things went badly wrong, by the force of circumstances, he would have to resign from his job. And so he had no choice but to try his adventure elsewhere. He had to leave the country in Africa to go to Europe. Finding himself abroad, jobless, without papers, he had to fall back and be taken care of by his wife. His wife was a blessing to him. She did not abandon him. She didn't try to make him feel guilty about why they got there. But she was very supportive, morally, physically and spiritually.

The people who were there as his friends, more and more, withdrew. Some family members who were helping him turned their backs on him. He could then see who was really who during that time.

To paraphrase the French President, **Emanuel Macron,** it is in difficult times that useful solutions are built.

It is true that the situation is different with the Ivorian, but from the little I have been able to observe, the conclusion is the same:

"The lemon is only important if it has juice."

In the family fraternity, friendly...

There are people who are very listened to, considered more than others in their family, because of what they have, what they own.

Especially in the daily life of Africans, we even see that sometimes, when there are problems, when the family is in trouble, they even decide to get together to find a solution. In this kind of family reunion, the voice that is most listened to is that of the person who is well balanced financially, whether he is the youngest of all or not, it is enough that he has a good social position, he would be listened to by the rest of the family members.

This is even very much in evidence in festivals, churches, conferences, assemblies. Better seats, very often in front of the podium, are only given to people who have paid better, to people who have a good reputation, a good social position, to people called ''VIP'' (Very Important Person).

What do you do when the lemon runs out of juice?

When you feel rejected in society, abandoned by your own, neglected. You feel like you're no longer considered. Your voice is no longer listened to, your suggestions are not given much consideration. Take your pain in patience, know that the lemon is important only when there is juice.

Remember that the company will only give you space if you have something to offer.

Whatever the situation, stay focused, stick to your goals. Remember that the people around you will only see the consequences but will pay less attention to the causes of things.

The world around us does not take the time to reflect on what made a person act in such a way, but will always be ready to criticize and sanction the consequences.

People will take less time to worry about the things that caused you to run out of juice, they'll tend to just throw you out.

Whatever the case, don't lose sight of your goals.

Don't let the people you meet in your life pull you down. Do not be so discouraged when you find that you are surrounded by people who are not true, but hopefully, confide in one or two true people around you who will always want your happiness, for angels exist.

Some will stay with you for various benefits. Some will come into your life just either to have the children with you, take your name and leave, others will come to secure and change their social status, others may be to use the intelligence or the light that reflects in you.

No matter how a person comes into your life, if that bond is not bound by a deep desire of the heart, the relationship will never go far.

A Luba saying, a tribe at the centre of DR CONGO, says: "the needle picked up in the game, always gets lost in the game.

The beginning of a relationship will also determine its end. Knowing how to meet the right people, at the right time, in the right places, is the hallmark of successful relationships.

So, what to do? In your suffering, take the time to analyze your situation.

One of America's greatest thinkers, Vincent Paul Norman said, **"Every problem contains the seed of its own solution.**

It is a very good description of the process to be followed to solve a difficult
problem:

it is necessary to **Believe, to know, and to reflect**...In other words: knowledge, reflection, faith.

The beginning of the solution to any problem begins with **knowing the facts**. When we cultivate knowledge of ourselves, our values, our needs, our ambitions, the knowledge of people around us, their expectations, desires, fears and ambitions. The knowledge of the situation, of the environment in which we evolve.

We need to turn on the radar inside us to find out what is really going on in us and around us as we move towards the solution to any problem.

Then take some time to **think**. Reflect on the causes, consequences, and outcomes of any action we want to take. When thinking about making a decision, it is important to consider the technique called **"Whole body decision"**. This technique requires that we take into account all the important parts of the body in order to finally make a good decision.

In decision making, the "**whole body decision"** recommends that we use our brain, heart and intestines.

The brain: is the part of the body that allows us to reflect on the facts, to consider what is real, logical, rational, consistent. The brain is the centre of reason. According to US Army research, a soldier who uses his brain in the field of operation, is lucky to have 70% reason for making these decisions. While 70% for a soldier who must avoid bullets, attacks from the opponent, this percentage is not enough.

The heart: is the centre of resentment, feeling, vibration. The heart is the part of the body that has a strong impulse of electromagnetic force. It has been shown that the heart can communicate, feel the impulses on the 608 meter around you. The heart can feel fear, joy, strong emotions, positive or negative. In making the decision it is necessary to be attentive to all these emotions but also to be able to tame them.

The intestines: are in the belly where we feel fear and instinct for things. We often feel fear in the belly. The intestines in the belly have the same shape as those in the brain. It's like having two brains, one in the belly and one in the head.

The "**whole body decision"** recommends that we pay attention to the influence of all these body parts, not just one, in order to make a correct decision.

To be correct in decision making, only reason, only feelings or only intuition are not enough. You have to consider the whole picture.

I mean, I guess so. You have to believe the miracle exists. You have to believe that anything is possible, even at the last minute. We have to believe that there is still hope to return to the job market, to return among people in good health, to return among people we can trust again. We must believe that the end of everything will always be better.

Knowledge, reflection, and belief are the basic keys to the solution of all our problems.

Give her life meaning again, have a new dream.

"*Life's too short to be small*" **Benjamin Disrael**.

You can't end up where you've never seen yourself before.

To get your life back on track, you have to dream again, set new goals.

Martin Luther King's **"I have a dream"** is timeless. No one will ever know where he didn't want to be in his life.

You have to dream, dream and dream some more, while at the same time setting goals, deadlines, actions to be done. Knowing that a dream without action is just an illusion.

People who succeed and solve their problems know that there are two kinds of habits to avoid and two kinds of mistakes to be ashamed of.

These habits lead right to failure: **procrastination and weak-willed.**

Procrastination: this is when a person always puts off until tomorrow what he has to do today.

To be Weak-willed: It is when a person has many ideas, many projects without realizing them. He chains ideas together. Every day that passes, he has a new idea, even though he hasn't yet executed the idea or the Project he had first.

I remember a friend from university, very smart, passionate, and gifted in all things IT. He had a very beautiful idea to design a game show, a model genius in the making, a question for a champion, which was to involve all students and pupils of the city of Kinshasa, in DR Congo. The game had to have the participation of a major television channel and have the sponsorship of a national company. While he was in the middle of the process, some difficulties arose, while he was trying to solve these difficulties, so he was inspired to create another project, leaving the one he spent time on, he was already thinking of starting another good idea on cartoons. Neither idea has been completed, this is the result of a vague desire.

But once he makes the decision to go all the way, based on one idea, one project. There will be nothing to stop it and there will be no failure.

It is important to note that no matter how many good ideas and good projects we may have, if we do not take action, it will be useless. No success can only happen on the basis of dreams, or good intentions.

Even hell is full of good intentions, they say.

How do you stop to be weak-willed?

There was a young man who had finished his studies, after several attempts, he still couldn't find work. Discouraged, he came to see me in my office. At that time, I was director of the Employment Assistance Service of an autonomy centre.

So this discouraged, unmotivated young man said to me:

'' Mr. Director, please get me a job. I'm doing everything I can. Nothing succeeds. Even when the door is open for everyone, I just have to get to this place, then they close the door on me''.

I say to this young man in these words:

My role is not to find a job for you, but to help you to do something to find a job and become independent''.

Then I add this:

''If you want to be self-sufficient, you have to stop being a quitter.

I've seen you animate very good ideas, very good intentions, but you can't bring them to fruition one by one.

Earlier you had decided to do an English course that you started and didn't finish. Afterwards, you thought about doing driving school because you thought that learning to drive would increase your chances of finding a job quickly. You did the driving school theory, but so far you're having trouble passing your test and getting your license.

I'll give you a recipe, which I think will work for everyone, what **Tim** Ferris, American writer and businessman, calls the **Chrono-Dream.**

It's about limiting your dreams in time and space. A simple and effective method that anyone can do".

Then, I asked the young man to make a list of the 5 things he must do for the next 6 to 12 months. I asked him to ask himself these questions to identify the things he had to do:
What 5 things do you dream of having in the next 12 months?

What are the 5 qualifications you dream of being in 12 months?

What are the top 5 things you dream of doing in the next 12 months?

This principle of "**Chrono rêve**" is really based on having a clear vision of where you want to be in the next 12 months.

What we want to own, be, and do. Then we set these objectives to be achieved.

In the process of accomplishing something, we tend to be afraid to make mistakes when we should never avoid making them.
There are two types of mistakes we can all make.

The first is **a mistake of ambition.** This mistake is made when we are motivated to achieve something, to act. Because we lack complete information about what we want to achieve, we can make this mistake. It is difficult to have all the information we want, so lack of precision, lack of important information can lead us to make mistakes of ambition. This mistake is to be encouraged. As **Ingvar Kamrad says, only those who sleep do not make mistakes.**

The second mistake is the one to be avoided. It is **the mistake of laziness.** This is made when we avoid doing something out of fear, out of ignorance, out of too much illusion. When we avoid evolving and leaving a negative situation when we had all the information we needed to move forward but want to remain in the status quo. It is by commenting on this mistake that many people remain in poorly paid jobs, miserable marriages, unproductive relationships.

Let's summarize some of the principles listed in this chapter :

1. *Lemon only matters if it has juice.*
2. *This world is a meeting place of giving and receiving.*
3. *Sometimes it is hard to realize with bitterness that you will only be important if you have something important in your hands.*
4. *We're either loved or we never love for anything. There's always an interest.*
5. *Successful and problem-solving people know that there are two kinds of habits to avoid. These habits lead straight to failure:* ***procrastination and being weak-willed.***
6. *Practicing the principle of* **Chrono-Dream**.
7. *It's about limiting your dreams in time and space.* A simple and effective method that anyone can do.
8. The ''**whole body decision**'' recommends that we pay attention to the influence of all parts of the body, and not just one, in order to finally make a correct decision.
9. To be correct in decision making, only reason, only feelings or only intuition are not enough. It is necessary to take into account all of this in its entirety.
10. Two kinds of mistakes, mistakes of ambition and mistakes of laziness. The first not to be avoided, the second to be avoided.
11. Ingvar Kamrad: "Only those who sleep do not make mistakes.

Chap. 4. Get rid of the things that clutter up your life.

We devote our lives to what we devote our time to. Here on earth, we are subject to time. We also have free will, and we can do what we want with our time.

William R. Bradford.

"Nature abhors a vacuum."

Throughout our days, everyone's main activity is to fill our voids, to fight boredom.

The man feels bad about doing nothing. We always find something to do. Either we watch TV or read a book, when we're done we want to go for a walk, as soon as we get home, we have the phone in our hand that takes our attention.

Especially the smart phone and social networks are taking up so much of our lives. Someone said, we are living **the "head down generation**" with our smart phones.

Everywhere on the street, in meetings, in church, in the subway, you will always find people who have bowed their heads in chatting, truly a "head down generation".

So we have our heads down, even figuratively, we can easily get lost on the road, bumping into each other in what we do.

In this world full of noise, full of occupations, distractions, incomprehension, it becomes more and more difficult to find time for oneself, to meditate.

We all tend to do something every minute.

"Nature abhors emptiness."

Even an empty house would have spiders that would occupy it if it remained empty for too long.

It's true in itself, nature doesn't like a vacuum. Even a woman or a man who has been alone for a long time finds another alternative to fill this void. If he or she wants to remain faithful to his or her partner, virtual love can act as a palliative.

Unfortunately we are around intense noises, we get lost.

The history of the inhabitants of Athens shows this so well, in the Acts of the Apostles where it is written: **"Now all the Athenians and foreigners living in Athens spent their time only telling or listening to news"**.

The people of Athens, who met to get news, had become more interested in things that did not solve the daily problems of their lives. But they were more open to sensational news, news that struck the eye. Although they met and shared news with each other, there were more noises that prevented them from discerning what was really for their own good.

When the apostle Paul passed among the people of Athens... His message focused on the resurrection of Jesus Christ. When the crowd understood the religious nature of his message, some mocked him, others rejected him simply by saying, **"We'll hear about that another time**.

So they had no time for what seemed irrational to them when deep down they could save them. Paul left Athens without success.

Dean Fréderic Farrar wrote about this visit: "**He did not found any church in Athens, he did not write any epistle to the Athenians, and although he often passed through the vicinity of Athens he never set foot there again. »**

Man is only attracted to news. All the time, he wonders, what's going on around us again? What's the news in America, Africa, Europe? But sometimes we consume more noise than things that are useful for our lives. We clutter up our lives too much with things that are not important.

Our daily duty before going to sleep is to always ask in all these noises that have surrounded the day, what have I learned?

Like the People of Athens, I grew up in a neighbourhood called Mama Yemo, in Kinshasa, DR Congo. When we were young teenagers, we had a place where all the young people of this neighborhood met almost every day around a big stone called "**Berlin**". All of us young people from this neighbourhood were called **Berliners**.

We spent a long day discussing like the people of Athens all around this stone. We were also very concerned about some news.

One after the other. Young and old. Most of us came back from school in the evening, we all gathered there, discussing various topics of society: music, sports, general culture, politics, etc..

Sometimes we would stay late at night, making noises, the parents would come and disperse us to go to sleep.

We young people of that time, now we're parents. We are fondly remembering the beautiful moments we spent around the Berlin Wall.

This wall also had this positive side where beyond the pleasure of meeting each other, we learned from each other. Some of us came from good families, went to very good schools, and could come back and share what we had learned in school with us who came from modest families and did not have the same means to go to the same schools. Around these noises, we were able to share knowledge that later served us well in life.

Most of these young people were from Berlin, a district of Kinshasa, which had nothing to do with many other districts of the big city, but at that time we were ahead of the game in many areas. We were a force of youth. There was no subject that was set aside, from politics to religion, from sport to social facts. The Berlin Wall made us all, for the most part, executives in various areas of society. We are currently scattered all over the world, but we still have good memories of our childhood around this Berlin Wall.

Around the noises that surround us, that clutter us daily, we must ask ourselves certain questions that should allow us to organize our lives.

What do I have to get rid of to free my life from what's cluttering it up?

Sometimes we surround ourselves with very useless things around us. Either old pots and pans that we no longer use, an old car body in the plot, clothes we no longer wear that we could put back in the charity shops but we hang on to them.

Even further away, we have some friends who are useless to us and just clutter up our lives.

We're surrounded by music noises, media information, we take an interest in certain hobbies that really clutter up our lives.

First, get rid of the information that's cluttering up your life.

There are many things a wise man may wish to be ignorant of," said ***Ralph Waldo Emerson.***

Developing selective ignorance

The first thing that clutters our lives on a daily basis is ***the media.***

Whatever its form, online media, print and audiovisual. They clutter up our lives.

I'm a trained journalist myself. For more than five years I had to work in this profession in television and the written press. So I do not intend to minimize this job.

I'm just siding with consumers and trying to suggest what could be better to do amidst the noise of this media whirlwind.

Amidst the media noise of the newspapers, news in briefs that are broadcast every five minutes on our radios, our televisions. We must always ask ourselves, does it matter to know everything? No, it doesn't matter.

It's pretty important to know about everything that's useful in our lives.

We must develop selective ignorance. Get rid of useless knowledge.

To get rid of the media noise that clutters our lives, we must instead apply **selective ignorance**.

This notion of **selective ignorance** advocated by Timothy Ferris, a famous American author, encourages us *to put ourselves on a dry diet of information.*

Sometimes it is not necessary to know everything.

An event helped me to better understand this principle in everyday life. One day, I got a phone call from a friend. She was sobbing. She was crying and she didn't even say a word. The sentences she was uttering were barely coming out. Everything I heard, she said, Russell, he did it.

I tried to ask, who did what, but she insisted, your friend did. He cheated on me with another woman. I was speechless and listened to my friend. She told the little story. Then she kept crying. Although she was in pain, she said I just want your friend to tell me how many times he did it. Why did he come so far? What day had it happened? Where did they do it?

I told my friend directly, I understand that this is difficult to live through, especially for you to control yourself but rest assured, in this moment, these details will be of no use to you! They are not important.

I reminded him of the words of **Robert J. Sawyer** ***who said that learning to ignore things is one of the great paths to inner peace***.

Then the idea of Tim Ferris came directly to my mind. I told him, you know what can help you right now? She told me, what? I said, it would be difficult, but try to keep you on a strict diet of information about this incident. I advise you to be **selectively ignorant about** this event. Really choose what's useful to know. Otherwise, the more you know the details, the more it will hurt, and the harder it will be to pick up the pieces.

But I doubt very much she took that advice. Her heart was burning so badly that she wanted to know everything at all costs. Often, in the face of disappointment, we tend to do the opposite of what we are advised.

This example illustrates that when you want to know all the details about your partner's infidelity. It will not solve anything, but rather it will still drive the deceived one into deep anguish. Details in certain areas can kill you.

" The devil is in the detail," they say.

To return to the selective ignorance to be applied to the media. It is necessary to leave aside what is not important in the media. Don't bother to spend a lot of time in front of newspapers, television, radio, internet.

This time can be replaced by positive activities such as chatting with our spouse, going for walks and rides with friends, spending time playing with our children.

The news on TV, radio and the internet increases our stress. There is less and less good news in the media.

It takes time to diet the news.

Just turn on the TV and follow the morning news, you'll hear that there's a murder in such and such a corner of the neighbourhood, such and such a region of the world has been hit by the earthquake. One country is preparing to attack another.

Information workers are putting too much data on us, most of it from the wrong sources.

I'm not suggesting that you stay ignorant, or that you stay away from all the media, but in order to have a fulfilling life, less stress, you have to choose what is useful to consume in the media. The media clutter up our lives.

The flow of information and noise brought by the media increases our stress. And yet, **Dr. Hebert Benson,** of the Medical Institute of Harvard University, has stated that 80% of the sickness consultations he has done are stress-related, and 60% to 80% of occupational accidents are also stress-related.

Rid your life of what's cluttering it up to avoid stress. Get rid of cumbersome media and choose to live under selective ignorance.

Second, to rid your life of what's cluttering it up, revise your schedule.

"We devote our lives to what we devote our time to.

In this life, we are subject to time. We also have free will. So we can do what we want with our time.

Put aside everything that wastes time, such as useless phone calls, cats that bring nothing, sterile discussions in the corners of avenues, harmless relationships.

Then avoid anything that consumes your time such as repetitive tasks, unproductive meetings and visits.

Don't tolerate fools and imbeciles, you risk becoming one, as Tim Ferriss so aptly put it.

It is also important to ask ourselves What do we do in our spare time?

Get rid of the friends that clutter up your life.

There is a saying: friends are like books, you have to have few but good ones.

There are relationships that don't work out. Friends who don't raise us. Love affairs that have become almost toxic. Friendships that have become a burden to bear. These relationships clutter up our lives. We have to get rid of them. In other words, we have to get rid of them as quickly as possible.

Surround yourself with people who trust you, who believe in you, who can pick you out of the trash where you were to get the best you have and you are.

Identify the fewest possible friends who bring you more happiness, stick to the fewest possible friends who bring you fewer problems but contribute to more solutions to your problems.

By the time you read these words, just take a look at your phone book, you will see that there are over a hundred unnecessary contacts.

Just look at your Facebook account, Instagram, Twiter, you'll see that you had over 300 contacts who can't even buy you a $5 sandwich if you're hungry. You don't even have 50 safe contacts who can pay a $100 deposit if you're locked up somewhere. You may not have 20 safe contacts who can just make a simple phone call to comfort you when you are sick. You have to get rid of these kinds of people, they are unnecessarily cluttering up your life.

Get rid of the little demons in your life. Here, the little demons of our lives, these are the bad habits we have developed that can destroy us.

Pornography, sickly jealousy, drugs, violence, brutality, any kind of addiction can become our little demons that are difficult to overcome.

Every person has a lot of flaws but just a handful of strengths. To be able to fly away and blossom, you have to focus more on those few strengths. Make them improve rather than spending time doing them, redoing the same things, developing the same habits that destroy our personality, habits that don't allow us to fly away, behaviors that put our life and future at risk.

Get rid of the old stuff that's cluttering up your life. It is important to sort out our objects, materials, sort out what is necessary and what is superfluous.

We clutter up our lives with things that are no longer of any use to us, but we keep them out of nostalgia.

Just look around us, in our houses, our plot, our shops, there are tons of things that are no longer of any use to us. Things that are stupidly piled up and take up space unnecessarily. Things that prevent us from airing when we complain that we don't have enough fresh air. Things that clutter us up and make us prisoners.

The list is long, it can be an old Mercedes car parked in the plot that won't start for years, clothes that we no longer even wear, child dolls kept piled up when we no longer had small children at home, furniture such as wardrobes, black and white television from the 80s that you won't find spare parts anywhere.

It is only when we get rid of these things that we realize how distracting they were, how they took up space not only physically but also mentally.

It's important to always sort out things regularly that are no longer of any use to us but that we can give another person a smile with.

The T-shirt we no longer wear, once dropped off at a charity shop, can become a party outfit for a person.

There is an old saying: ***"What is nothing for one person,*** can be ***everything for another"*** (one's man nothing, can be one's man everthing).

The girlfriend (boyfriend) that we neglect, that we find he means nothing to us, maybe the woman (man) who means everything to the other person.

Just as we free up space in our phones by deleting applications, photos and files that are of no use to us, so it's important to free up space in our relationships, homes, old stuff and some of our habits.

Now that we have figured out how to get rid of the things that clutter up our lives, let's recap some of the ideas listed in this chapter:

1. We dedicate our lives, what we devote our time to. The quality of what you give your time to determines the quality of your life.
2. Nature abhors a vacuum. Be careful, there will always be something to fill it.
3. Get rid of the information that clutters up your life.
4. In the face of media congestion, develop selective ignorance.
5. The devil is in the details. Sometimes it's not important to know everything.
6. Get rid of the friends that clutter up your life. Friends are like books, you have to have few but good ones...

UPDATE HIS STATE OF MIND

Every man is where he is by the law of his being, the thoughts which he has constructed in his character have brought him there, and in the arrangement of his life there is no element of chance, but all is the result of the law which cannot be changed.

James Allen.

Chap. 5. For your own happiness, accept what you are.

"One can have affection for friends and the truth, but morality consists in giving preference to the truth".

Aristotle, In Ethics to Nicomacheus.

I'm compelled to share a personal anecdote. One morning, caught deep in solitude, alone in my room in a refugee house in England where I was housed. I had a time of deep meditation on the situation I was experiencing at that time. I found myself alone, away from my wife and children.

That morning, I had a very negative feeling about myself, which is very rare for me.

I woke up very sad that morning. I was thinking about some of the choices I'd made so far in my life.

I took some time to take stock of how old I was in my thirties. I had a wife and children who had lived almost five years away from me. I had just lost a very interesting job with a position of great responsibility. That morning I found myself in England in a nightmarish immigration process that I didn't know when I would get out of this maze.

I realized that throughout my life, I had no real friends that I could really count on. For many years, I was surrounded by people who weren't real. As a result, no one was there when I had a hard time.

I've thought deeply about some of the mistakes I made that put me in this uncomfortable position. Mistakes that could have cost my marriage, my faith in God, my health.

But with a little more reflection, I also realized that some of these mistakes were not just negative but brought certain opportunities and accomplishments.

At that time, I was having endless arguments with my wife that were ruining my days. Being far away from each other, these arguments were more caused by many points of disagreement that either she or I brought out.

After several analyses, in my torments, I found that the problem to my misfortunes was me. The only person to blame was me.

I understood that there were two things I had to correct in me: **My kindness and the way I deal with differences of opinion with others.**

I got out of bed quickly and the good news is I still had my life ahead of me. If I wanted to be happy for the rest of my sixty years ahead of me, I had to rethink the way I managed my relationships with others.

My overwhelming kindness came from the fact that in the functionalities of my mind, already through my education, I thought that my happiness should be complete only when I responded positively to everything that the important people in my circle (family, friends) asked me.

I was passionate about satisfying anyone who came to me with a problem. I did this until I lost my job because of a friend whom I had decided to help when it later turned out that he was not correct in his other relationships.

I needed to update my way of doing things and seeing things, to update some of the features in my mind.

In this chapter, I describe some of the steps I took to solve my problem to build my own happiness.

These steps can also help you.

For your own happiness, decide to be true.

I think the most important thing in our relationship with others is to be true.

Sometimes our system of thought invites us to be nice, more than to be true.

Sometimes we say yes when we should have said no. We kill ourselves to please the other.

Stop being nice, but be true'' is the title of a book written by **Thomas D'Ambourg,** a Belgian writer, psychologist and supporter of Non Violent Communication (NVC).

When I realized that I had to decrease my kindness, and become more and more real, I decided to attend several of this author's conferences, and read his book which helped me understand that I had to strengthen my ability to be real in my relationships.

Thomas D'Ambourg, answers the question of how one person can go against the other while remaining himself?

I understood that I could satisfy some of the demands of influential people in my circle and still be myself.

Most of man's misfortune comes from the fact that he has been too kind until he is not true, not being himself.

HEBERT Bayard Swope ***says there is no recipe for success but the recipe for failure is to try to please everyone all the time.***

In reading this quote, I really found myself in my past experiences.

With each passing day, many people lament having been used by ill-intentioned, manipulative, narcissistic, and other people. Many have put kindness forward and given the opportunity to the profiteers to use it as a weakness.

Whereas it is possible to love while being true, while being oneself. It is also possible to be loved while showing exactly what we are and want, rather than spending our time seeking at all costs the satisfaction of the other.

The kindness we're talking about here is the kindness of the facade, the kindness of the surface. While we want something else on the inside, but the outside shows something else.

The prudery and hypocrisy no longer work in these times.

This attitude not only harms the other, but harms yourself first.

I've decided to stop being nice and start being real.

Man develops in an environment that conditions us, conditions our spirit, our way of life and our way of doing things.

We have long lived with the fact that our comfort is conditioned by the satisfaction of others. Our relationships with others depend more and more on the satisfaction we give them.

Parents, on the one hand, threaten disobedient children with punishment, on the other hand, they condition gifts and other rewards on achieving better grades at school, on good behaviour.

Relationships between spouses centred around the incessant preoccupation of trying to satisfy the other's desire. My wife likes this, my husband likes that, my boyfriend told me if I hang out with this friend, he'll leave me.

We build our mindset around the satisfactions of the other sometimes to the point of forgetting ourselves, either for fear of being punished, or to do well in the hope of being rewarded, admired, praised and loved more.

While these forms of communication: punishment and reward carry the seeds of personality conflicts.

It has been shown that there is more violence in moralizing societies that promote the use of punishment against any wrongdoing.

Marshall Rosenberg, *founder of Non-Violent Communisation (NVC) explains it so well that in the processes of NVC it is in everyone's interest that people change, act not out of fear of punishment but to do so on the basis of intrinsic value, that they act because they have understood that their actions enrich their lives and those of others.*

I decided myself never to act again, either for fear of some form of punishment or reward, or not to make others feel it. It is more interesting when we rise to the level of doing our actions by our own free will knowing that these actions enrich our relationship and that of others.

These beliefs of satisfying the other to avoid punishment or gain reward condition our minds, imprison us. This way of doing things creates "fake people" which I prefer to use the English term "Fake people", hypocrites, fake relationships.

We only do what we do to satisfy the other rather than to be.

When we are only doing what we do to satisfy the other rather than being, we are, as **Thomas d'Ansembourg** says, in the **confines of** our system, our mind. (Note the word hell in bold.)

Being yourself. Be true. Being real.

The way our mind-is-set, our mind is formed **locks** us in. (Observe that he has the word hell in bold in this word).

Sometimes we say "**yes**" out of fear of not being loved when deep down inside we want a **"No", sometimes we** accept invitations from friends and neighbors when we wanted to spend our time differently.

This kindness of facade is at the base of infertile relationships, relationships with hidden agendas, unproductive relationships.

What's the point of waking up all morning and seeing the people we don't want to see? But we keep seeing them!

What's the point of continuing to do work that no longer brings joy? But we keep going!

How important is it to be in a classroom that we don't like the teacher or the subject? But we still stay there!

The reconstruction of our person passes by the assertion of oneself, to be true rather than to force kindness.

It is important to stop, to reformulate our beliefs, to decide to be true.

When we decide to rebuild ourselves, we have to change our habits. Revisiting habits is what is difficult for all of us to do.

In relational system analysis, it is said that if you do what you are always used to doing, you get what you are always used to getting.

Change is not easy, because men prefer to stay in their comfort zone, but what kind of comfort do you accept to stay there if it causes you trouble?

For your happiness, decide to be true!

For your own happiness learn to say "No", also learn to listen to "No".

Saying no is never a problem for me in relationships, but I always found it hard to accept being said "No", especially when I want something, when I want someone.

I just figured I can't have it all in life, too. You have to let some things go, let some things get away, let some people go, let some people escape.

Clinging to what has to go is to make yourself miserable.

It is important if we want to remain true, to sometimes have the courage to say no, or to listen to a no coming from others.

It is not enough to say **"yes" or "no"** in our communication, but we must take time to express ourselves, to motivate them so that the person in front of us understands that our motivation is not to oppose but rather to participate in the solution.

It is better to be an agent of solutions than to maintain problems.

When we accept things when we know deep down we don't want to, we choke ourselves.

Sooner or later it could get exposed.

This attitude of outward kindness creates illness in the person who maintains it.

Thomas D'Amsenbourg's expression puts it best when he says: "If **I repress** what would be right for me to **express**, sooner or later **it is printed**, and then **I get depressed**".

Depression is a logical consequence of worries, uneasiness, thoughts fleeing inside us that we refuse to externalize, thoughts about realities that we refuse to accept.

There are many people walking down the street with heavy loads that are not visible. These burdens are not carried over their heads but inside their heads.

Sometimes it's less heavy to carry something over your head than it is to carry it inside.

For your happiness, learn to say No, also learn to listen to No!

For your own happiness, take care to Feed the "We".

I met a friend who was in her forties, she was still single although she had a child. In the conversation, she explained why her other relationships had not worked out. I had noticed that several times she repeated this famous sentence: "I like this, I like that... With **me**, things must be like this... **My** principles are very clear in this or that field.....

I quickly noticed that she was more in her **"Self"** rather than accepting to go meet others while remaining herself. I try to make her see that the "We" also existed as soon as we agreed to be in a couple, we agreed to leave home and go towards others, we must also agree to feed the "We".

True people in relationships are those who prioritize the well-being of all by nurturing "the We".

To be true in a relationship, I'm not saying you don't care about the other person's needs or your own needs, but rather you go out and meet the other person's desire while expressing your own in order to find the right balance.

It is the management of the happy medium that allows a healthy relationship to flourish between two free and consenting adults.

In a real relationship, there's always compensation to be made. And when one is a free and consenting adult, one does it willingly, driven by love, self-esteem and the esteem of the other.

When we engage in any relationship, it is important to note that there is the presence and desire of three people to nurture.

There's **me,** there's **you, and there's us**.

- **The "I" is** our own identity, our personality, our temperaments, our needs, our behavior, with all that goes with it.
- **The "You" is the** person opposite, the group of people we lead, with all that goes with it.
- **The ''We'' was** born the day we met each other, the day we made the decision to walk together. For a leader, the day he took on the task of leading others, that's when the "We" begins.

When **the "I"** alone is more nourished in the relationship, **selfishness** will develop.

When it is the **"You"** who is much more privileged, satisfied, it increases **hypocrisy**. Hypocrisy creates a lack in the other who see his needs are not taken into account.

In the end, when it is the **"We"** that prevails, we build a fulfilling, lively and solid relationship.

The true high relationship is found at the level of **"we"**. This is where the source of any solution lies.

In a couple, when both spouses deliberately and consciously leave the stage of "I" and "you", and seek to nourish the "We", we will speak of a mature couple.

Likewise, when a leader is concerned about the collective **"We" of the** people he leads, in the society he serves, he will create an environment capable of successfully solving all of society's challenges.

It is at this high level of management that **Aristotle, in Nicomachean Ethics says**;

The good of the State is superior to the individual good of each citizen: the good is certainly desirable when it concerns an individual taken separately, but its character is more beautiful and more divine when it applies to a people and to entire States.

You're really a rich man when you create other rich men around you.

What use is it to a man to accumulate individually all the goods on his own, and around him he is surrounded by the poor? It is inhuman and far from divine.

The divinity resides in the **"We"**. In any relationship, actions, accomplishments, everything that is done in the interest of seeking the welfare of this **"We"** is more noble and praiseworthy.

It is at this level that we are called to review our Mindset, to review the way our thought system, our beliefs are shaped.

From an early age a man's mindset is shaped so that he pleases his parents, that he does good to the other, to his spouse to win his love, to adhere to his vision, in short to get a reward or to avoid punishment.

For those who are believers, many of them live their whole lives locked up, imprisoned, in fear of losing Paradise or being sent to hell after death.

This fear increases a large number of fear believers rather than faith believers who rely just on the intrinsic value that a life of discipline brings. Believers who believe just because the principles once applied can enrich life, not believe because they are afraid of either hell or heaven in the future.

When one is preoccupied with nourishing the "I" or the "you" alone, one is once again locked up in this system of logic that one must satisfy oneself alone or one must try to satisfy the other. This attitude easily engenders lies.

Lying comes when you want to protect yourself in the relationship at all costs, or you want at all costs not to lose the other person.

Some Mindset even agrees to use lies to make the relationship exist.

While surface kindness always has a lie for companionship.

Often lies take many forms. The lie can be expressed or not expressed, it can be verbal or accompanied by a mimic, a gesture, a look, one can even lie by remaining silent or by saying that part of the truth is true.

The one who is not true in a relationship will always use small and big lies to get out of it, he will feed his relationship only by tricks.

Sometimes when faced with certain situations he will say that he was forced to do so, to use a lie that can be considered a healthy lie to maintain the relationship, and save the situation.

The danger of this practice is that once one has lied, there would still be a succession of lies to cover the first one in order to keep one's front position. Right now we're more truthful in the relationship.

That's how there's more and more of a façade relationship, from the outside, while inside there's nothing more.

Once the decision to be true is made, keep it simple:

For your own happiness, learn to nourish the "We" in your relationship.

For your own happiness, don't always try to be right.

Whether we are right or wrong, sometimes to save the relationships that mean so much to us, all we have to do is say the words **"sorry", "I apologize", "I admit my fault"**.

In reality, it is still not easy for most individuals to have the ability to humble and recognize themselves.

We are fuelled daily by this desire to win the battle.

This is where we talk about managing differences, welcoming differences in others.

Our mindset hardly tolerates disagreements.

The other trap that prevents a person from not being true is when there is a difference of opinion, when there is a divergent point in the relationship.

One is tempted to either impose one's opinion in order to be listened to, one can even use force, violence, to impose oneself.

Either we simply decide to satisfy the other even when we think the opposite in our inner self, we are afraid of losing him or her, we are afraid that the relationship will end, and we prefer to bow down.

When you bow down, you're no longer real, you put yourself in a self-sabotage situation. We even risk allowing a relationship of submission, domination, flogging to take hold.

Our mindset hardly tolerates disagreements.

Thomas of Amsenbourg said even adults often confuse disagreements with love.

We think that since the other one does not agree with my opinion, since he does not want to adhere to my vision of things, he does not like me.

As I said at the beginning of this chapter, as a young married couple, me and my wife had gone through a period of great tension, of arguments.

Sometimes the subjects of these disputes were trivial but important to one or the other but were not seen in the same way.

For example, for me, I found it very bad that a married person stays in contact with one of his or her ex-boyfriends or girlfriends, whereas for him or her, it was no problem at all.

We had differences of opinion on the use of social networks, on some religious principles, on employment, we had to decide whether she should accumulate jobs when we had small children. These subjects divided us at times.

My mindset being forged by a highly patriarchal society and tribe. . . From time to time my gulp tightens at the idea of listening to him give an opposing opinion. From time to time I tended to want to be listened to at all costs. Luckily I never resorted to force or anything similar.

But after the help of non-violent communication, I realized that there is the me, the you, and the We that I had to build. I had to sit down and listen to the needs and motivations for all the arguments on both sides. I had to welcome differences even when I disagree. I had to put up with listening to a contrary opinion even if it is a subject that is more valuable to me.

It is true that even today, some points of divergence may appear, or may exist, but I quickly learned to welcome the difference of the other through active listening, patience, serenity, compassion, and empathy.

Once in our little domestic dispute, she said to me:

''Can't you see we're different in a lot of ways, maybe we should split up?''.

I replied:

''Of course, it's because we're different, that's why we have to stay together to complement each other. I continued, in a humorous tone, saying:

''Imagine how you'll feel if you're wearing a pair of shoes with both feet the same.

It is diversity that makes the very beauty of a nation, of a country. It is in the diversity of colours that the beauty of a rainbow lies''.

So in the process of rebuilding our beliefs, of actualizing our state of mind, we must insert this aspect of reformulating our mindset by learning to welcome the difference of the other, to sit down and listen to the other.

It is important to internalize empathy, which is a form of active listening. A person who listens with empathy puts himself in the other person's place, does not judge, does not condemn. He simply has time to listen without showing that he is in a hurry to move on.

Once empathy is imprinted in our minds, it allows us to reach out to the other, creating an environment that will foster the creation of solutions for the "**We**", rather than monopolizing the word and imposing ideas.

For your own happiness, don't always try to be right.

The imposition of his opinion can give free rein to emotion.

FOR YOUR OWN HAPPINESS, DETACH YOURSELF FROM EMOTIONS.

In order to welcome the difference of the other, **one must detach oneself from emotions.**

It is not easy to listen to a contrary opinion on subjects that are really close to our hearts. It is difficult to remain insensitive, not to react.

Feelings of anger, jealousy, animosity, doubt can overwhelm us but it is important to detach oneself from these emotions.

When we react emotionally, we don't solve problems. Emotion does not produce ideas, but rather it produces effects.

After an emotional reaction, one partner often chooses to cower. He or she chooses to exclude himself or herself from the round table discussion. They exclude themselves from any kind of conversation. Not feeling understood, he may choose to keep quiet and simply shut himself out.

Out there, keeping silent about important matters is like death.

Martin Luther King said, *"Our lives end the day we decide to keep silent about the serious things around us.*

To paraphrase him, I would say that any human relationship dies the day we start keeping silent about the serious things around it.

When communication is cut off, it is an open door for partners to open up to other people we think are always listening to our problems. It can be a friend, a boyfriend, a service colleague, a neighbour, a former lover. Often these people are not far away. They are always hanging around. Often ready to be of service.

When we leave ourselves to others, little by little another new parallel relationship may develop. The person in need of a relationship soon feels like a person who has found an oasis in the middle of the desert to quench their thirst.

Others manage this situation well, come out without incident, but many have let the parallel relationship lead to other openings, create other problems. The parallel relationship may consolidate the main relationship, or it may even devastate it.

Of course, the reactions differ, for some people. For such, when the difference is not welcomed, the person prefers not to broach the subject anymore to avoid again arguments, reactions under the emotions. He prefers to sabotage himself, to destroy himself by accumulating within himself all these emotions that can be a source of illness later.

Staying away from emotions doesn't mean creating a distance, keeping quiet, not bringing up the subjects.

Staying away from emotions allows you to manage disagreements with coldness, calm and serenity.

Even when disagreements are insurmountable we can coexist without going to war. This is only possible if we do not suppress dialogue. It is possible that if non-violent communication becomes an important part of our daily lives.

Marshall Rosenberg, one of the founders of nonviolent communication gives us a choice by saying:

''We have the fundamental choice in life, it's to be happy or to be right.''

I hope that everyone would choose to be happy in their relationship by going against the other while remaining true to themselves, avoiding superficial kindness, especially by staying away from emotional reactions.

Several principles and ideas have been developed in this chapter. Let's summarize these ideas:

1. In our relationship with others the most important thing is to be true.

2. Most of man's misfortune comes from the fact that he has been too kind until he is not true, not being himself.

3. Man develops in an environment that conditions us, conditions our spirit, our way of life and our way of doing things.

4. The way our **mindset,** our spirit is formed **encloses** us. (Note again the term **hell** is in bold in the word).

5. It is better to be an agent of solutions than to maintain problems.

6. *In relational system analysis, it is said that if you do what you are always used to doing, you get what you are always used to getting.*

7. It is not enough to say **"yes" or "no"** in our communication, but we must take time to express ourselves, to motivate them so that the person opposite understands our position.

8. True people in relationships are those who prioritize the well-being of all by nurturing "the We".

9. For your own happiness, don't always try to be right.

10. When we react emotionally, we don't solve problems. Emotion does not produce ideas, but rather it produces effects.

Chap. 6. Discover what is little but much in you.

''You don't have to do extraordinary things to get extraordinary results.''

WARRET BUFFET.

Modern life seems in some ways to be a mistake.

The good things that modern life brings us are the wonderful advances we have made in science, technology and business. These advances have allowed us to eat better, to stay young longer in the world, to move very easily through high-speed trains, to connect the world as if we were in one village, to enjoy more comfort than past generations.

But the modern mistake is in the way we organize our personal and social life. Instead of working to live, we lived to work. We spend so much more time in work that we forget the essence of life.

In this area, we can say that technology has hurt us.

Other times, people had a calmer, more balanced life. They had more free time. They were more committed to family and friends.

There was more fraternity and social equality, more civility towards strangers. They suffered less stress and depression, less dependence on alcohol and drugs. They were less obsessed with money and power.

Today we are more aware of ourselves and our individuality, but this new freedom terrifies many of us.

We are much more worried, and we are desperately seeking the illusion of security, which, despite our frantic efforts, seems to be slipping away all the time.

In today's modern life; people are faced with making choices between two lanes: ***the fast lane (speed) or the slow lane.***

Both of them have much to envy the ***wide track of*** other times.

For many people, ***the slow lane*** means financial insecurity, low incomes, the bottom end of the social ladder, fear of unemployment and the loss of the material pleasures enjoyed by people on the fast lane.

The ***fastest*** route, however, is not without its pitfalls. For many people, it is a path that rhymes with devouring ambition; it requires them to invest fully in their professional lives, to the detriment of their personal relationships.

On this last path work takes up more space on everything. The faster path also brings with it a lot of anxiety and poverty, although in this case it is not material poverty, but poverty caused by lack of time and love.

In order to get more money, more recognition, a more interesting job or a more exciting life, it seems that you have to invest more in your profession, your job, your company or your clients, sometimes to the point that you no longer have time to take care of yourself, your family or your friends, let alone to relax and recharge.

Many of the things to which we devote our energy are not only useless, but also harmful.

We are observing the lives of young people nowadays, they spend almost all of their day on social networks, while they can read, visit museums, have real conversations with their friends next door, their parents, their brothers and sisters. But alas, they prefer to go on social networks to unknown people, at distances that they hardly know except virtually.

In virtuality everything is beautiful. Imagination amplifies the facts in the virtual, while on the other side we realize immediately that it was only a chimera. Once you see the person in front of you, you realize that his or her appearance was accentuated by the fraudulent use of make-up and photos modified by modern smartphone applications. We immediately realize that the person was better on the close-up of a well targeted body part that they chose to show rather than seeing it in its entirety.

With the speed of social networking, ***"Kalaba, the witch"*** can turn into "***Beyoncé***".

In the virtual world, just a simple voice from a person you have never seen can get you attached to that person until you are caught up in reality.

It's all about speed in this life.

The reality is that modern life is materially, scientifically and technologically efficient, but it often wreaks havoc on people's personal lives.

In this modern life people often run after things they already have without knowing it.

***The history of fable and adventure hunters shows us*:**

This story is about what happened between an American businessman and a Mexican villager.

Once upon a doctor's order, an American businessman went on holiday to Mexico, to a small village by the sea. Awakened by the multiple calls of his work, he decided to take a walk along the coast to exchange ideas.

He took a look, he saw a small boat with a fisherman on board, and in the boat there were several large yellowfin tuna fish.

The American complimented him and said:

''How long did it take you to get them?

"Not too long," replied the Mexican in impeccable English.

"Why don't you stay at sea longer to catch more fish? "asked the American.

"I have enough to support my family and give some to friends," says the Mexican as he unloads his peach in a basket.

"And the rest of the time, what do you do then?

The Mexican lifts his head and smiles: "I get up late, do a little fishing, play with my children, take a nap with my wife, Julia, and every night I go to the village, drink wine and play guitar with my friends. I have a rich and full life, Sir".

The American bursts out laughing and bursts into laughter: "Sir, I have an MBA from Harvard and I can help you, you should spend more time fishing and, with the profits, buy a bigger boat. In no time at all, you could buy several boats. And you'll end up running a fishing fleet. »

He goes on to say: "Instead of selling your fish to a middleman, you would sell it directly to consumers, and eventually open your own cannery. You would control the product, the processing and the distribution. You would then have to leave this small village, of course, and move to Mexico City, then Los Angeles and, why not, New York, where you will find the right skills to continue to develop your business. »

The Mexican fisherman then asks, "But, señor, how long is all this going to take? »

To which the American replies, "Oh, fifteen to twenty-five, tops."

"And then, señor? »

The American laughs and says, "This is where it gets really interesting. At the right time, you go public, you sell your company's capital and you become very rich. You'll make millions.

"Millions, Señor? What's next? ».

"After? You retire and settle in a small village by the sea, where you sleep late, fish a little, play with your children, take a nap with your wife and go for a walk in the village in the evening, drink wine and play guitar with your friends... " (Stories from the book at 4:00 a.m. weekdays)

Men very often run to the things they already have without knowing it.

And yet happiness continued to come from appreciating what you already have," says Congolese rapper ***Gims Gandhi Djuna,*** *"And yet happiness continued to come from appreciating what you already have.*

That's where the fast lane takes us. The American, who believes in the fast lane of this modern world, proposes to this villager to run, to work more, to earn more diplomas, to look for more than a million at the cost of sacrificing his wife, his children and his health, to finally return to the starting point where the villager was already.

While the villager already had the little that gave him a lot. He worked for little time, but earned the essentials to support his family and friends. He worked in a short time to live in a wide way. The wide lane that had the good fortune to spend more time with his family, at the seaside, in a quiet little village, around his friends sharing a bribe with friends.

This is the happiness that all those who live on the fast lane of the modern world hope to live after a long period of work of more than forty years in order to live their retirement in a small village by the sea. A retirement that is not so guaranteed. A life that can be cut short at any time by illness, accident, or any kind of life's ups and downs.

The Bible reminds us of this in these words:

"Now it's up to you to say: Today or tomorrow we'll go to such and such a city, we'll spend a year there, we'll hunt, and we'll win!

You who don't know what will happen tomorrow! For, what is your life? You are a vapour that appears for a little while, and then disappears ". (James 4:13-14).

Steve Jobs' advice before he died.

Steve Jobs *is one of the wealthiest businessmen of our time. At 23, he already had $1 million in his bank accounts. By the age of 24, he already had 10 million, and by the age of 25 he had over 10 million.*

Shortly before his death, Steve Jobs confessed that money is not the most important thing in a person's life. He said that money is important because it allows him to realize his ideas, but for him, he found that what is most important in life is human relations in society.

In his sickbed, shortly before his death, he said these last words:

I have reached the pinnacle of success in the business world. My life is an example of success. However, outside of work, I have had little joy.

After accumulating enough money for the rest of one's life, we must pursue other goals that are not related to wealth. These Objectives are of great importance for example: art, history, our childhood dream...

In life, memories that have been strengthened by love are the true riches. Love can travel thousands of miles. That's how life has no limits. Go wherever you wish, do your best to achieve the goals you want to reach, everything is in your hands.

You should know that the most expensive bed in the world is the sickbed.

You, if you have money, you can hire someone to drive your car, but you can't hire someone to take the disease. Lost material things can be found, but there is one thing you can't make up for once you lose it, and that's life.

No matter what stage of life we find ourselves in, in time the curtains will fall. Give importance to family love, love for your spouse, love for your friends, love for your children, take care of yourself".

How important are these words spoken by Steve Jobs before his death. He lived a life of great speed, and accumulated everything a man could have; success, wealth, fame.

But at the end of his life he invited the world to follow the wide path, the path based on the little that gives us more in life.

What is the good news, to compensate for this reality, to stay happier, to achieve great results in one's professional life, and at the same time to have time for one's social life as well.

The right path to a larger, more spacious, happier life is to identify what is little but much in you. To achieve this, you must live these two principles:

- ✓ **the 80/20 principle, otherwise known as Pareto's Law.**
- ✓ **The principle of Biens Heureux's life by creating mini retreats.**

Pareto's law.

Wilfried Pareto, is an economist and sociologist who lived from 1848 to 1923. An engineer by training, he began his professional career managing the coalmine quarries, and later succeeded Léon Walras as head of the chair of political economy at the University of LAUSANE, Switzerland.

His major work, Cours d'Economie Politique, included a "law", then little explored, on the distribution of income which would later take its name from the "Pareto Law" also known as the "80/20 principle".

Statement of the 80/20 Principle.

The 80/20 principle can be summarized as follows: 80% of out puts are produced by the 20% of inputs. We note for example:

- 80% of the consequences arise from 20% of the causes.
- 80% of the results come from 20% of the effort and time.
- 80% of a company's profits are generated by 20% of its products and customers.

There are many examples in all aspects of life that demonstrate this principle:

- Less than 20% of artists receive more than 80% of the Public's attention.
- In politics, 80% of war problems in Africa are caused by 20% of the population who claim to be a minority.
- Similarly, the Chinese make up only a third of the population in Malaysia but hold 80% of the country's wealth.
- Americans represent less than 5% of the world's population, but are responsible for 50% of global cocaine consumption.
- Less than 20% of recorded music plays more than 80% of the time.
- Less than 20% of the war causes more than 80% of combat deaths.

Professionally, the 80/20 principle teaches that a minority of tasks leads to a large majority of results. So, if we know what we want to achieve, we can look for a hyper-productive way to do it.

That's what makes a good manager, a good worker. It is only profitable when we identify in our job description, which 20% of important tasks bring 80% results. Remaining, less urgent, less important tasks can be delegated.

By doing so, we can have more time to think, find new strategies, be more and more efficient.

The 80/20 principle ensures that there is always a way. Always to do more with less, as long as you recognize the 20% of people, methods and resources that are particularly imaginative and productive.

The objective is to identify your inefficiencies in order to eliminate them and to find your strengths so that you can multiply them.

The principle of 80/20 can be summed up in the concept of **Doing More with Less, which is in other words identifying what is less but gives you more.**

Doing more with less.

This principle of "doing more with less" is very important and must be applied in one's professional life rather than in social life.

In our personal life, there are always things that bring us a lot, but require little money or effort.

Saying thank you, showing gratitude or affection, admiring a sunset, taking care of an animal or a plant, smiling at a casual acquaintance or a stranger, being kind to someone, taking a pleasant walk, these are all ways of doing more with less.

These activities do not cost a huge amount of money but bring us more pleasure, more joy. Thus, the reward is disproportionate to the effort made.

Doing more with less'', i.e. knowing or identifying the few highly productive forces and methods (the 20%) and multiplying them in order to obtain the best results while spending fewer resources.

The principle of "doing more with less" is based on the law of **concentration**.

Concentration is the power of all happiness and personal success. Concentration means doing less, being less, focusing on one thing, one target, one goal.

In reality, by concentrating on one thing, you make the reduction, ignoring all the others, but you gain more.

It is because of concentration that "less equals more".

Concentration requires us to focus on the best of you and you will find that less equals more.

This requires a new way of thinking which can be summarized as follows:

Animals are able to work hard, only humans are able to think hard.

Human civilization was not built by hard work, muscular strength, repetition or long hours of labour, but by intuition, inspiration, invention, originality and enterprise.

The most successful people don't change the world with the sweat of their brow, but with ideas and passion. It's not about hard work or endless hours, it's about vision. These people have original ideas that express their individuality and creativity.

Thus, to be successful, one must think and act accordingly.

Do you believe that **Bill Gates**, who dropped out of university to launch Microsoft, became the richest man in the world by working hard? Or did he just have several genius ideas while thinking about how to solve life's problems?

Do you think that, **Warren Buffet**, the 89 year old Master Investor, who has US$86 Billion in fortune in 2019, is working very hard?

Can you imagine that ***Jeffrey Preston*** Bezos, the current Billionaire and the richest man in the world, the CEO and President of Amazon.com, do you think he works from morning to night in his office? Or is he just thinking about an idea that can make a difference in the marketplace?

And what about big media stars like the Cardashans? What's so special about them? Are they workaholics or do they have original ideas?

Barack Obama? Ronald Reagan? John F. Kennedy? Kofi Annan? Albert Einstein? Christopher Columbus?

Not all these famous men are people who chain themselves to the office. They're just looking for ideas that will set them apart from the rest. They work on what matters most. They know how to delegate where to delegate. They put a lot of time into what really mattered to them.

By discovering what is less and gives more in you with the 80/20 principle you will be able to focus on results, to concentrate on what matters more.

This principle asks us to focus on what produces more extraordinary results without making extraordinary efforts.

Be efficient but relaxed'' Think first of the result, then focus on getting it with as little effort as possible but identifying the right person, the right resources, the right method to get it.

Stop spreading yourself too thin and doing everything just because you can: it makes you less efficient.

Focus on the really important activities that give you extraordinary results.

"Don't work hard, work smart.

Most entrepreneurs have never attended university or even college. More than half of them left school as soon as they had the opportunity to do so. Their enthusiasm, their passion, is the reason for their success.

Take a good look at what succeeds in their field are those who have a good command of a given sector. They do not scatter.

Take football stars like **Lionel Messi, Zinedine Zidane, Cristiano Ronaldo, Mohamed Saleh, Samuel E'too, Didier Drogba, Sadio Mané,** or even other NBA Stars like **Mutombo Dikembe,** the famous **Michael Jordan.** They have succeeded in their field because they are specialists in what they do.

They spent several hours of training to master a technique, either dribbling, attacking or defending.

Very big stars have very big strengths and very big weaknesses. Their weaknesses matter little compared to the extraordinary results they achieve by focusing on their strengths, which they cultivate at an Olympic level.

It is important to have general knowledge, but it is even more important to excel in one's chosen field.

By discovering what is less and gives more in you with the 80/20 principle you will be able to focus on results, to concentrate on what matters more.

This principle asks us to focus on what produces more extraordinary results without making extraordinary efforts.

Be efficient but relaxed'' Think first of the result, then focus on getting it with as little effort as possible but identifying the right person, the right resources, the right method to get it.

Principle of life for HAPPY GOODS.

Then, the other principle that allows us to follow the broad path of life to be more balanced, enjoy more space, and be fulfilled while working is the HEALTHY GOOD lifestyle.

This way of life defined by TIM FERRIS, an American author, encourages people to focus on the essentials in their professional tasks. They don't have to wait until retirement age to enjoy the fruits of their labor, but instead, it encourages people to take time off from work, rest, travel, spend more time with their loved ones.

The happy ones are the people who have managed to set up a system that runs and produces their money without them being present, so the machine runs for them, and they enjoy having a good time, family, friends, in the things that give more joy of life.

Happy Goods are not people who confine themselves to an office and do 8 hours of work, but the sooner they create employment, they undertake, take on more important tasks and delegate others.

Now that we have covered this chapter on discovering what is little but much in you, let's recap some of the ideas developed in this chapter:

1. You don't have to do extraordinary things to get extraordinary results. Keep it simple and you'll get more results.
2. Modern life offers us two paths to follow, the fast path and the slow path, but we have to find the balance by following the wide path.
3. Men often run after things they already have without knowing it.
4. The most expensive bed in the world is the sickbed. Enjoy every moment of life. What is most important is family love, love for one's spouse, love for one's children, love for one's friends, and take care of yourself.
5. The Pareto Law 80/20 states that there are only 20% of things that give us 80% happiness, joy. What is the 20% that distinguishes you from others? What are the 20% of key activities that you need to concentrate on to get more results? What are the 20% of skills you need to master that will bring 80% success in your life?
6. Stop being generalists and become specialists.
7. This principle of "doing more with less" is very important and must be applied in one's professional life rather than in social life. There are always things that bring us a lot, but require little money or effort.
8. Many of the things to which we devote our energy are not only useless, but also harmful.

Chap. 7. Download software for your brain and mind.

Man is always the master,

Even in the weakest or most abandoned state.

JAMES Allen.

One day I was sitting in my Bishop's office, a young man came in to present me his grievances. For several months he tried to find a job, but unfortunately all his efforts were in vain.

After listening to him, I then shared a lot of job search techniques with him. How he could introduce himself when he has an interview. How he could make a strong impression in interviews, and also how he could effectively network to get more job offers.

In spite of all the efforts made to give these explanations, the young man looks at me and says:

''Bishop, leave it, you're worrying about nothing. "I've found that every time there's an opportunity, no matter how easy it is for other people in my house, it's hard, even when the door is open for everybody, but once I move on, you'll see the door is closed.

I looked at the young man silently, after a moment's reflection, I said:

''Your problem is in your mind and your brain. You're like a computer with a virus, you'll have to clean it and download some software to work properly''.

After this remark, I shared with him some principles on the impact that there is between our thoughts and our actions, on certain limiting beliefs, some of the self-prophecies that can be harmful to ourselves.

Here I am talking about downloading software for the brain and mind that will shape the way people live.

A software program is a set of programs, procedures necessary for the operation of a system.

Our brain is a complex system that allows man to think well, speak well, act well, communicate well and adapt well to his environment.

As part of personal development, I think it is important for everyone to download effective software for the proper functioning of their brain.

This downloading can happen when we attend a conference, we read a book, we participate in a teaching, and at the end of it all, we manage to print these thoughts in our brain, and our mind so that it constitutes software that will influence our thoughts, our way of communicating, our way of life.

Metaphor of the Brain and the Computer...

The Frenchman, **Steve Abd Al Karim,** an expert in behavioural science, uses the computer metaphor to illustrate how the brain works in our lives.

We are each equipped with **a computer at home or at the office**. Very often, at the time of purchase, no one has had the time to read the instructions or manual that comes with that computer before using it.

Then, in order for the computer to serve us with a large capacity, we must install Windows software such as WORD, EXCEL, POWERPOINT, etc.

Afterwards, very often, if we are not careful, our computers are affected by viruses that slow down the speed of RAM.

To protect them, you buy or download anti-virus or other software to secure your computer.

Same as **our brains.** We're all born with brains. We're all born with brains. It is the center of our life's activities.

Paul Vincent Norman pointed out that the only function of our body is to support our brain.

So everything we have as body parts, arms, legs, stomach, are in the body to support our brain.

From birth, when we are endowed with a brain (which is compared to a computer) our mothers did not teach us how to use it to its full capacity (they did not read the manuals, instructions for our brain).

And yet there are trainings, techniques that can teach us how to use our brain properly.

As we said above, to use our computers properly, we program Windows software such as Word, Excel, PowerPoint, etc.

Just as our brains direct our lives, we need to download software into our brains to function properly and influence our lifestyle.

For a positive life full of fulfillment, it is important to download software such as :

- ✓ **Positive thoughts.**
- ✓ **Helping beliefs.**
- ✓ **The power of speech.**
- ✓ **Non Violent Communication (NVC).**
- ✓ **Negativity Management.**
- ✓ **The power of Positive Thinking.**
- ✓ **Very important managerial applications.**
- ✓ **An Application of how to present yourself well in the business world, etc...**

This list may not describe all possible side effects.

This list of applications to download into our brains, into our minds, to cope with life is very long.

Unfortunately, unfortunately, our brains can be infected with multiple viruses. These viruses can be:

- ✓ **Certain limiting beliefs that prevent the person from progressing.**
- ✓ **Afraid to make mistakes.**
- ✓ **The impulse.**
- ✓ **Procrastination.**
- ✓ **Negative self-prophesies about yourself such as ''I suck... I can't do this... I can't do this... there's no job in this town, I'm a mother and fatherless...**
- ✓ **Negativity.**

All this thinking can slow down the speed of our self-realization.

They can constitute an obstacle to our development.

Someone who often uses this kind of language, simply programs his failure.

For example, the one who says **"how stupid I was that I was"**, if he has **speech power antivirus** software in his brain, that software will directly replace those words with **"I should have made better use of my potential and my intelligence**" there, the brain implies that one is intelligent.

Let's give a quick overview of each of the software we offer. Here I give you a summary, but each person is asked to look for books, authors, conferences and teaching of each principle discussed finally to download this software in your mind or brain.

Speaking of downloading the software, we invite you to immerse yourself in these principles, to live it in your daily life, to wake up with it, to house it in your deepest subconscious.

A brief overview of the Positive Thinking software.

There are several authors who can help to influence and manage thoughts.

But I suggest the one that has had a strong influence on my thoughts is James Allen's "**As a men thinketh**".

Once we download this software into our brain, we will understand the influence that thoughts have on our whole life.

Man is what his thoughts are.

James Allen has made it clear that **thoughts and behaviour are one**.
We only act the way our thoughts are.

Thoughts are the seeds from which behaviour sprouts. Just as maize seeds can only produce corn and not peanuts, nettles only produce nettles, just as our behaviour is only reflected in the thoughts we have.

We are not sad for nothing, we do not develop aggressive behaviour, all this reflects our inner thoughts.

Just as on the other side, a person with an attitude of enjoyment, tranquillity, serenity, simply reflects what is in the depths of his thoughts.

We can't have unhealthy thoughts and feel good about our surroundings.

Just as we cannot enrich thoughts of being kind to one person and then behave badly towards the same person, so we cannot enrich thoughts of being kind to one person and then behave badly towards the same person.

Thoughts are the seed from which behavior sprouts. Just as maize seeds can only give corn and not peanuts, and nettle seeds only give nettles, so our behaviour is only reflected in the thoughts we have.

David O. McKay said, "*We sow our thoughts and we reap our deeds; we sow our deeds and we reap our habits; we sow our habits and we reap our characters; we sow our characters and we reap our destiny*".

(C. A. Hall, The Home Book of Quotations, New York: Dodd, Mead & Company, 1935, p. 845.)

Thoughts create circumstances. Sooner or later, what we think will happen in our lives.

For those who have understood this profound truth of mental strength, which is the power of thought, they develop a great capacity for self-control. They do not allow any thought to be maintained or developed in their minds, because they know that sooner or later what we say and think will eventually happen in our lives.

Thoughts have an effect on circumstances. We invite circumstances of good or evil with our thoughts.

I saw this principle in the life of a friend I knew in college. She had had a rather turbulent youth. She dated many of her married friends whom she saw being unfaithful to their wives.

Later she married herself to a man who lived by Christian principles, very exceptional, and of high morality.

Despite the qualities of her husband, the girl in her thoughts, she always told herself that one day her husband would cheat on her like most men do.

Her thoughts created circumstances, a trip happened, the girl was away from her husband for a while and in an unexpected way, her husband stayed in a circumstance that he ended up cheating on his wife with another girl. This happened after many years of faithfulness, but the wife had in her heart the thought that her husband will always cheat on her one day.

Thoughts bring the circumstances to become favourable for those we imagine, good or bad.

Illness, health, death, behaviour, circumstances are rooted in our thoughts.

Thought has an effect on the human body.

Job said it well: "What I fear is that which befalls me; what I fear is that which befalls me" Job 3:25.

Fear and dread in our minds poison the blood, and create death faster.

The person who thinks about an illness, ends up getting sick.

Continual critical thoughts often produce rheumatism. Tumours are caused by thoughts of jealousy, hatred, refusal to forgive others, fear. Every disease or discomfort is created by an uncomfortable state of mind.

Thoughts animated by the refusal to forgive offenses is the most common cause of many diseases, sclerosis of the arteries, liver, and eye diseases.

We've all had to think about death, to wonder about death. This fear of death poisons the blood of human beings that causes us all to die one day at a time.

Some religious leaders died very early because they were too haunted by the thoughts of knowing what happens after this life, what happens after death. The more we think about something, the more it will happen.

It is important to look for other applications mentioned above to guide our behavior, our brain and our mind.

For the summary of this chapter, here are some ideas developed :

1. Here I am talking about downloading software for our brains and minds that shapes the way people live.
2. Everything we have as body parts, arms, legs, stomach, are in the body to support our brain.
3. From birth, when we are endowed with a brain (which is compared to a computer) our mothers did not teach us how to use it to its full capacity (they did not read the manuals, instructions for our brain).
4. Someone who often uses negative language simply programs his failure.
5. Man is what his thoughts are.
6. Thoughts have direct consequences on behaviour, body and circumstances.

Chap. 8. Managing the factors that can affect our personality.

"Change brings opportunity.

Nido R. Qubein

These next two chapters will help you discover what kind of person, of people, you are. Also, it will allow you to find out the kinds of people around you.

In this eighth chapter we will talk about what causes a person to become negative.

And the next chapter will look at the kind of person we are surrounded by in our professional environment. These people can be our leaders, our supervisors, our colleagues.

There would be no question of transforming these people, no longer have to flee from it, but we will see more how to deal with these negative people who ignite our daily lives. How to live with them without becoming like them.

In this book we talked about how to deal with people negativity in our work environment, but let's remember that the family is the first society where we are called to be employed for the rest of our lives.

Whenever we talk about the company or professional environment, you can replace the bosses by your parents or spouses, and colleague by your brothers and sisters.

It has been more than fifteen years since I followed the teachings of an American lady, a lecturer and famous author, Zoie Kaye.

The way this lady demonstrates how we can say No to negativity has had a big impact on the way I think, on the way I act. These teachers have transformed me profoundly. Ms. Zoie, although she didn't know me, but these writings, these lectures helped me discover who I was.

Negativity management is an important element in our process of rebuilding our lives. It helps us to understand who is around us, how to eliminate negativity in ourselves.

Once we understand how to manage negativity we can manage not to change the people around us, but we can manage them and have ways to cope with living with them.

In this book, I will make a reminder of these principles of how to say No to negativity, how these experiences have helped me personally.

First of all it is important to address **the factors** that lead a person to become negative such as: **the effects of a load, the economic situation where we live, as well as family contexts**.

The effects of a change in life.

Every day we are called to live with the challenges that change brings to our lives.

I had to facilitate a training workshop on self-reliance, among the participants there was a war-wounded soldier who had lost his leg. This change in his physical appearance profoundly changed his way of seeing things, he had become totally negative in his language and vision of seeing things. He was worried at all times about his relationship with his wife, about his authority towards his service colleagues, about his importance to still be of service in society. I found that this change in his physical appearance had a strong negative influence in his life.

Just as man must eat, wash, sleep, and seek to meet all the vital needs to sustain his life, so too must man eat, wash, sleep, and seek to meet all the vital needs to sustain his life. Just as much as change is a natural fact linked to our experience.

Whether we like it or not, a man necessarily undergoes a change in one area of his life.

This change can be seen as an opportunity for some, and can also be seen as a threat to others. No matter how we take it, life will be full of challenges related to change.

The change in our personal and family environment does not leave us indifferent.

It can be a break-up with your fiancé, a divorce with your partner, the death of a friend, an illness that occurs and paralyses you, an accident that affects your whole life, infidelity of a spouse, all these unfortunate events leave no one indifferent.

It can also be a new job, a new degree, a new love relationship that makes our hearts beat faster, a new country to discover, a change in the work environment, these happy events in someone's life do not leave them indifferent.

No matter what kind of change we make, it affects our attitude and our way of life.

But, we must remember this:''***Changes bring opportunities''*** observation made by ***Nido R. Qubein,*** *A motivational speaker, Businessman, Lebanese American, President of High Point University since 2005.*

But for the cynics and the Negatives, even nice things happen in life. For them they see the arrival of these events as a source of unhappiness.

For example, a wife with negative feelings, even toxic; she may complain about a second car her wife buys. She will only see this car as a source of infidelity for her husband for whatever reason.

In the workplace, changes in your work environment can affect your attitude, either positively or negatively, such as the arrival of a new boss, the announcement of a staff reduction decision, or the arrival or hiring of several other employees who must now work with you.

Whatever the change, let's not resist, but rather live with it! Change is part of our lives, change will always happen, let's live with it, let's deal with it!

The economic situation.

Increasing financial burdens can also be an element that can turn us into a negative, toxic person.

As soon as I arrived in Europe, the first constant I made around me was that people were complaining about the long list of bills they had to pay at the end of the month.

Each stage of life brings with it certain financial burdens to bear. When we are single, living alone, the financial burdens are different. Once we are married, it also becomes different. And when the children arrive, the financial burden increases as well.

We didn't have a car, we like to take public transport, whereas we can get to the city, as in certain circumstances public transport can be a little less expensive. Once you buy a car, you think you are solving a problem, but the pressure of bills increases, insurance, vignette, technical control, maintenance, etc..

In this modern life with financial overload, both men and women have to make the effort, both working away from home to make ends meet.

They face multiple bills to live and maintain their homes.

If one is not well prepared, this change of seeing the two of you as a couple going to work can create either a negative attitude of resistance, a threat to the stability of the couple, or a door to arguments.

Whatever the case, financial burdens affect an individual's attitude. It can make him angry, skeptical, negative, toxic, and discontented.

Some family contexts :

Certain family contexts, certain lifestyles can accentuate our Negative attitude towards life.

Easily the people who live the realities I will quote below, are likely to have a negative attitude in their lives.

1. Living in a "sandwich generation.

The term "sandwich" refers to a loaf of bread with several ingredients stacked together. A An element that brings several things together within it.

So, we talk about living in a "sandwich generation" when several generations live together in a house: parents, children, grandchildren who are children's children, older children who have children in the same house who still live in their parent's home, are being cared for by the same parents.

Often they face terrible financial situations.

This context of life easily creates the "Negativists", the "Embittered". Among these people living in the context of there will be more malicious people. Sometimes even living together in the context of a "sandwich generation" creates a climate of unfair competition between siblings, especially on ephemeral, very banal things in life.

Don't be surprised when you visit a family living in the "sandwich generation" and find two children fighting over a tablespoon!

Promiscuity promotes poverty. Promiscuity creates bitterness.

2. Living with "crab syndrome.

By putting several Crabbe in a bowl, we will notice that the Crab trying to get out is quickly pulled down by the others behind him.

In the family context where several family members depend on a single working person. This one person is in a situation where he or she has to take care of parents, siblings, friends, cousins, new.

And if they also have their own family, they will also have to feed their partner and children.

The only independent person in the family is like the crab that tries to get out of the hole but can't because the loads, the others, also pull him down.

Often this situation can affect either the person themselves or those around them to lament at any time because they do not feel fulfilled.

Worse still, those in his charge, who expect a lot from him, feel that they are receiving crumbs. They feel they are entitled to even more than they are getting.

The context or way of life in ''Crab Syndrome'' creates frustrated, dissatisfied, rebellious people. All these categories of people are part of the family of "Negativists", people who become toxic to others.

Unfortunately, it can be seen that people in developing countries, third world countries, Africa, South America are more exposed to living in these two contexts of family life.

Now that we are at the end of this chapter, let us summarize the ideas in this chapter:

1. Change brings opportunity.
2. Whether we like it or not, a man necessarily undergoes a change in one area of his life.
3. In the workplace, changes that occur can affect your attitude, either positively or negatively, for example the arrival of a new boss, the announcement of a decision to reduce staff, or the arrival or hiring of several other employees who must now work with you. It is important to be prepared for this.
4. *Whatever the change, let's not resist, but rather live with it! Change is part of our lives, change will always happen, let's live with it, let's deal with it!*
5. Increasing financial burdens can also be an element that can turn us into a negative, toxic person.
6. Certain family contexts, certain lifestyles can accentuate our Negative attitude towards life.

Chap. 9. What kind of man are you? What kind of leader leads you? What kind of colleagues surround you?

I worked for several years in a company that had a strong structure based on respect for hierarchy, internal rules and regulations that were worth much more than anything else.

So there was a tendency for some bosses to be more concerned about the tools provided for service such as vehicles, petty cash, meeting times, etc. The use of these tools, attendance at meetings were more important to some bosses than the people we served.

Having been motivated more by the 80/20 principle, other result and performance based principles, I tended to focus on the more important things that would make a difference in what the company had to offer. For me, the vehicle of work, the meetings were only means to achieve the result, they were not the end in my eyes. So from time to time there were small misunderstandings about the use of the means at my disposal to accomplish my work and the way I had to follow certain instructions.

I quickly understood that in order to better keep this job, to be in harmony, I had to know the type of leader I had, the colleague around me and know myself, in order to manage the situation properly.

In companies, just as in our families, we are surrounded by people who like to impose their authority, some see things as bad, other goods recall the rules of the company, of the family more than the good being of people who even constitute this company or this family.

Now that we understood that certain situations can turn us into negative or toxic people. It is important to look inward, to examine ourselves, to determine what kind of person we are, what kind of people around us, colleagues, brothers and sisters.

Also, what kind of leaders lead us? Parent, husband, wife, etc.

To begin with, to better understand ourselves, we will talk about three types of people. Looking at a scenario, it will be easy for you to find out if you are :

An optimist, a pessimist, or a negativist.

When something happens, how you react can determine the type of people you belong to. -

Below is a scenario. As you read this book, picture this scene for yourself, and ask yourself how you will react to this situation.

'' You have a good, stable job, good salary, paid vacation and many other benefits.

One fine morning, you walk into your workplace, sitting comfortably in your office, your boss comes in and says, ''Sir, we are very happy with what you are doing as a job, but I am very sorry to tell you that things are not working out in the company as we would have liked. You've done a good job, but unfortunately we have to cut back on staff, we'll keep the ones with more seniority.

We'll keep you for this month, at the end of the month we'll pay you your salary, also an end of service certificate that you can use to find a job elsewhere''.

What would be your reaction?

Stop reading, think for a moment, write down your reaction, then go back to the reading, find out what kind of person you imagined you would react to.

A lot of people were faced with this dramatic situation. As long as you work for people, it would be important to expect this kind of situation one day.

Faced with this change, this event that suddenly arises, there are many different reactions depending on each individual.

Others have found it to be a dramatic situation, the end of the world, an apocalyptic event with no way out.

While some people, who I think are in the minority, have found it to be a temporary situation. This minority of people may find this situation as a source of 'openness to other opportunities may be even greater.

Let's analyze, some types of reactions and people, keeping in mind that in front of a glass half full, it will be seen differently by several people. Some will see it as a glass half full, and others will see it as a glass half empty.

The Optimist:

An optimist is a person who sees life's setbacks as a momentary situation. He actively seeks the positive even in misfortunes, he embraces to look for other possibilities.

The prison was a blessing for Joseph of Jacob's family.

An optimist doesn't give up, doesn't give up. He continues until his goal is reached.

He may even shout in his unhappy situation, the saying that somehow unhappiness is good.

An optimist, in front of this morning's scene, may take time to cry for a few minutes if he has to, but don't be long in standing up and finding the rose behind that thorn.

The pessimist:

It is a person who sees this change darkly, gives up easily, feels unable to overcome the situation.

A pessimist may not even accept the situation even though he knows he is the author who made it happen. He easily indexes the other even for his mistakes.

Good news for this category, for a pessimist the situation may seem like a "challenge" but after a lot of thinking, a lot of thought, and so on, a pessimist can get out of the situation, but this can only happen after many efforts.

The negativist:

The worst reaction is that of a negativist. The negative person would think that no matter what he or she did, nothing would work.

The negative will first look for the wrongdoer and take it upon himself, and will believe that the situation has happened because of such and such a person.

When a challenge arrives, he gives up easily, he sees that there is no solution in all directions, he looks for a bête noire, someone responsible for his situation and remains in misery.

According to Zoie Kaye, Ultimately, the way you perceive things around you can determine your attitude towards others, towards yourself.

Also, our way of reacting to a situation either optimistic, pessimistic, or negativist is created very early in your life, perhaps from a young age, but circumstances, events that happen to us can make us change our attitude either we become positive or we remain negative if we have been.

Types of people in the professional world.

Now that you know yourself, now see what kind of negative people you're dealing with and how to deal with them.

We'll talk about the kinds of leaders you might have in your workplace, but also about the kinds of colleagues around you.

As mentioned above, the same observations can be applied in your families

Type of chef

We will discuss five types of chefs that can be found in a professional environment. But this theory applies to any person who grants himself a piece of authority over others. In the family setting, this can be a spouse, a parent, an elder.

1. One Chief (Boss) Negative :

Most people work with a boss and say to themselves, "If only that boss could change the way he works, things will be different in this office.

Negative bosses are people who never accept their mistakes, they always blame other people for their own mistakes they have made.

Possible solution: With such a person, it is difficult to say exactly what to do, but the solution would be to develop a strategy that will allow you to survive with them.

2. The "stingy" or "stingy" chiefs:

A stingy boss when he comes into the office, he doesn't greet anyone, he doesn't smile.

The first thing that comes out of his mouth is, ***"I've never seen an office like this before. We're really behind everyone! I don't think things are gonna get any better in this office.***

Possible solution: With this kind of people, don't try to argue or argue, the right thing to do is to keep a good distance from the little you can. Stay the best you can on the subject to propose.

Very often, all day long we will end up finding out what made this leader's attitude negative.

3. The Chiefs "Yes, but...

Have you ever walked into your office with a big idea, you're too sure of yourself, and you tell yourself these ideas once accepted and implemented, things will change greatly in this company.

Already with this idea, you see yourself promised ''Vice President of the company''.

A few minutes after the conversation with The Boss, he tells you: *it's a good idea, but we already tried something like this 10 years ago but it didn't work, I'm very sure that even today it wouldn't work.*

If you fall in front of this kind of reaction, you have to ask yourself This resistance of the leader means what?

Does this chef want me to sell more?

Very often, this resistance of the leader can be a test, just to see if you master the subject, the idea you present.

Ask yourself, are you prepared enough to defend your ideas?

Possible solution; With this kind of leader, you have to resist a little. Present your ideas again with more impact, strategies. It can just be a question for the leader to know how serious you are in what you propose, he just wants to push you to argue more with passion and enthusiasm.

If you know you're working alongside a chef who's a ''**Yes, But**''... always be more prepared in what you offer. Talk about things that haven't worked before and demonstrate how your idea will fill in and move things forward.

4. The chief ''Tragic-Drama''...

This kind of leader, everything's tragic, everything's dramatic. Even a small incident for this leader is always serious.

In front of a situation, for example you are chosen to make a delivery at 4:00 pm but you did it at 4:03 pm. For this leader, this situation can be tragic and serious. Even if the impact of the action may be ephemeral, for him it can dramatize it

Possible solution: Often you will have too many threats when working with this kind of leader. You will feel too much pressure on your back, but whatever these words and threats, in front of such a tragic leader, ***keep calm, don't panic.***

Do not try to stop him or justify yourself while he is speaking, it would only add to the tragedy.

5. The Perfectionist :

A perfectionist leader himself is not necessarily a negative person, but he can simply create a negative atmosphere in the company.

They are from people who expect everything to be done right, not just by you, but even by himself. It is a person who, even when everything is well written, he detects and looks for either a comma is missing, or an "iota" is missing.

I worked with a chef who was like that. I remember, all the correspondence proposals, my emails, even when I took care to review several times, and when everything was perfect, there was always either a comma, an accent or a period missing.

When I returned from a trip on a service mission, I had bought a curdled milk at the airport during my stays in a foreign country.

It seems that the price of that curd was a few cents more than we usually knew, and that was just because it was at the airport.

*When he approved my bills and my travel report, he just went on to the one bill and shouted, ''**Russel, what expensive curds?**''.*

It made me laugh but a little discouraged by the fact that he didn't even appreciate at first the sacrifice and work I had just done but just the one downside of the curdled milk bill caught his attention to feed his hunger for perfection.

Luckily, I knew him. I knew he wasn't actually a negative leader, nor was he ill-intentioned. He was just driven by a sense of perfection.

So I was not affected by the situation.

Possible solution: The best way to work with a perfectionist leader is to ask a lot of questions, make sure you understand what he wants from you.

Type of Colleagues.

Now that we had the idea of the kind of leaders, parents, spouses we can deal with, and how to find the solution.

It would also be interesting to see the types of colleagues we may have at work, friends around us or siblings in the family.

Zoie Kaye distinguished several types of colleagues that I will simply summarize in three categories that interest me more:

1. The Grouch:

The grouch is the kind of person who, for example, just sits in your office. You're always waiting next door for a colleague to say:

''I don't know how I can stay at this job, I tell The Boss that this project won't work, the tools and machines we use are old and archaic''.

That wailing scream you wait for them day after day. Every moment, he's just bitching about it.

Possible solution: We just have to ask ourselves: Does this colleague know how negative he is?

There are people who have grown up in a negative environment, a pessimistic environment, and who have forged their character to the point of becoming negative without knowing it, if you have a personal relationship, try to talk to him about it and motivate him. By listening to him, you will be able to know where his negativity comes from.

2. The manipulator:

It's a person who sees others as pawns in a chess game.

They begin to diligently monitor the work of others. They create situations according to their moods. Their main weapon is intimidation. They like to make others feel that they are worthless, that they are not capable enough to do what they have been asked to do.

Possible solution: When faced with the proposals of a manipulator, simply say to him, "Thank you".

Thank him for his concern for you and tell him that you will do your best to do your job as you know how. Don't give him the opportunity to feed off your little arguments.

3. The Victim:

The colleague "victim" can be summed up in these laments: Why me? Why is everyone picking on me?

When you listen to these complaints from the "victim" colleague, the first impression is to sympathize, and yet this is the wrong thing to do.

The more you sympathize with him, the more he'd be more sympathetic to his complaints.

Possible solution: With a victimized colleague, listen to him carefully and help him to solve his problems himself.

Let's recap the chapter:

1. We will talk about three types of people it will be easy for you to find out if you are: **An optimist, a pessimist, or a negativist.**

2. When something happens, how you react to it can determine the type of people you belong to.

3. We will discuss five types of leaders that can be found in a professional environment: **negative leader, stingy leader, yes-but leader, perfectionist leader, tragic-dramatic leader.**

4. *It would also be interesting to see the types of colleagues we can have at work, friends around us or our brothers and sisters in the family, we talked about 3 types: Grumbling, **Victim, manipulator**.*

Chap. 10. Don't put yourself in the position of a loser.

"Making, making mistakes corrects more than explains."

Come here, Vicariah.

In society, we observe that there are classifications at all levels, some are first, some are second, and some are last.

No matter what the rank, no one loses.

Sometimes the difference between a winner and a loser is only attitudinal.

ATTITUDE

"Attitude brings altitude."

Whether you've been looking at life as a game or a fight, when the game hasn't come to an end yet, know that no one can call themselves a loser in advance.

In a fight as well as in a game, we can feel led, threatened, attacked, sometimes we can even feel we are already losing, but since the game is not yet over, there is no evidence that we are losing.

The only thing that makes the difference between a loser and a winner is attitude.

For football lovers, they are used to supporting their team until the end of the game.

How it wouldn't be the same for our own lives or the lives of others.

Loyal fans know that even two minutes of regulation playing time can change everything, either giving victory or defeat to his team.

Just as people full of faith, hope, positivity, and determination to succeed know that everything can change in their lives even before the last minute of their death.

I learnt that lesson in 1998, when my country, DR Congo, played Burkina Faso.

In 1998, the African Cup was played in Burkina-Faso. The teams had to face each other for the small final.

The highly motivated Burkinabe team, played on their soil, all the advantages, all the chances were on their side. They had the fans as well as their ancestors behind them.

Throughout the match, the DR Congo was threatened by 4 goals to 1.

In the second half, both teams returned from the changing rooms. The DRC were coached by a man called **Watunda Prof,** a very dynamic and disciplined man. Also the team benefited from some talented young players. Most importantly, these young people did not accept defeat easily.

Among those players were Emeka Mamale, Korando Kasongo, and Jerry Tondelwa.

The DRC players decided to come back on the scoreline, and it was in the last three minutes that everything was turned upside down. DR Congo were able to equalise by scoring three goals in three minutes. As a result, the game went into extra time, a penalty shoot-out, and so the Congolese team was able to win the mach and was awarded third place.

The match between Burkina Faso and DRC in 1998 has never been etched in the memory of this African people.

One wonders what really happened in the minds of these young players? What justifies the loss of the Burkinabe team? The answer is quite simply: **attitude**.

"Attitude brings altitude," they say.

The same scenario occurs several times in the meeting between the two best current big teams in the world, Real de MADRID and Barcelona. Any team playing against these two teams knows that as long as there is still a minute left to play, the game is not over yet.

What makes the difference between the players of these formations and those of the others? Just attitude.

By our attitude we can show whether we are winners or losers.

Our mind is the centre of all victory, all success.

Faced with a problem that looks like a mountain, what to do about it? We can only do it mentally. The invention of new technologies, and other conquests in the world, all this is created first mentally before being materialized.

We are born with a mind that gives a perfect attitude capable of realizing all that we can. This is why a child, encouraged by his parents and kindergarten teachers, always believes that he is capable of doing everything and becoming everything he wants in life.

The more we grow up, the more our minds are affected by environmental moral pollution.

We can't avoid making mistakes. Mistakes are normal facts in the process of a person's development.

Discover your identity

"Don't compare yourself to anyone, if you do, you insult yourself."

Bill Gates.

American author, comedian, and journalist **Dan Greensburg** said, *''If you really want to make your life depressing, try to compare yourself to others.*

How true that expression is. Comparing yourself to others makes you unhappy.

Others begin to compare their appearance with that of a friend, a movie actor, a sports star.

Or they begin to compare themselves to others in terms of achievement, in terms of the accomplishments that their neighbours have made. You could say, my father at 25 years old he already spoke 4 languages, was married and already had children, while I didn't yet.

Or we often hear these kinds of complaints. My child, with whom we finished university two years ago, has already found a job, while I'm still hanging around.

All these comparisons with others are only very good ways to make our lives more and more depressing.

Each person is unique in this life. Each individual has his or her own mission to accomplish.

Throughout life, the person is called to find what **Paulo Coelho,** in his **book The Alchemist,** calls: **The Personal Legend.**

It's important to find his personal legend, his mission early on.

In order to do so, we will have to ask ourselves this question, among the 6 billion human beings on earth, do I want to **be an addition of humanity or a contribution of humanity?**

- **The additions of humanity**: this is the category of people who do nothing with their lives. They don't take any risks. They have no plans, no dreams.

The additions of humanity complain and lament too often. They have only come to accompany the others. To use a harsh term, or not gallant, are people who are considered failures of life.

The additions of the earth are for the most part people who live in "airplane mode". They put their lives in airplane mode. When a phone is in airplane mode, it receives no connection, no incoming or outgoing calls. It doesn't download new applications.

Likewise, a life in airplane mode is sweet, withdrawn to a corner where one is content with photos and applications already found in the phone. No study project, no professional project, fear of committing to a relationship, in short, we are in airplane mode.

- **A contribution to** humanity: this is the category of person who has succeeded in contributing to do something in life that improves the lives of others.

In many ways someone can be an asset to society. They are teachers, doctors, writers, taxi drivers, bus drivers, waiters in restaurants, cooks, business leaders.

In short, those who wake up every morning with the spirit of improving someone else's life.

The classification being long in this category, individually, one must find one's personal legend, one's mission in society.

In this category there are those who are considered to be **great "contributions to humanity"**, such as inventors, creators of currents of thought, liberators, etc....

A person - the contribution of humanity - carries out his mission with joy. It's not enough to have a profession and say it's your personal legend. But the personal legend requires more than that, it must be a passion for you, a job that you feel deep down inside that you were born to do just that.

The Frenchman, **Steve Abd Al Karim,** an expert in behavioral science, says that **"contributions to humanity" that** succeed in their personal legend go through this formula:

Try - fail - succeed.

They forget the notion of loss and failure. They try, fail, try again and fail until they succeed.

The key to success for **people - contributors to humanity** is to try many times until they succeed.

Only 5% of humanity achieves this in terms of success, money and intellectual potential.

The rest of 95% of humanity gives up after a failure, does not accept any more risks, gets tired and gives up.

As an anecdote, **Thomas Edison,** the inventor of the light bulb, said that he didn't have a thousand failures before he succeeded in creating the light bulb, but that he managed to find a thousand ways not to make a light bulb.

So, his 1,000 trials and failures were just the road to his success.

There is no light without shadow.

Mistakes and failures prepare for certain success.

David Goggins, an American motivator, stressed the importance of making continuous efforts even after failure.

He says in his lectures that it is so easy to succeed today because most people are weak. We are in a generation of "soft" people, people who like easy. If you have the least tenacity, the least discipline, the least ability to do things that you hate to do, on the other side is success.

Anyone who has succeeded in creating his personal legend, his mission in society begins with **a dream.**

We must look to the future and see ourselves doing something fabulous, bringing an incredible solution to humanity.
Write this dream on paper, in a painting, on a wall, or in a closet, or even more, write it in the back of your mind. Imagine what you will be, and what the world will be like when you realize your dream.

The people who contribute to society make their way very early on. They set goals. They know which path to take.

When you don't know which way to go, you won't get anywhere. We'll turn around and finally realize that we've come to nowhere.

Imagine you get into a taxi, the driver asks you where you're going? And you answer: drive, I'm not going anywhere, I'll find the place while you're driving.

Imagine the energy that this car would consume, the tiredness that this driver will have while driving around in circles. And finally, you'll come to nowhere from your destination.

Therefore, it is very important to define the destination of one's life from the start. Very early in life, at a young age, one must find one's dream, one's destination, one's personal legend.

As Stephen Covey says, of the 7 habits of successful people in life, one is to see the end from the beginning!

Then you have to find your personal power. Each individual has a power that makes him or her unique. To find the personal power that sleeps in each person, to connect with this divinity that lies within us.

This power can be the ability to touch the hearts of others, the power of the hand to heal others, the potential to be always there when others are in good. It may be the ability to think more quickly than others, the gift of seeing more solutions rather than problems.

Search, search, search until you find that power within you. That will allow you to do what only you can do better than others.

Find your personal legend.

What category are you in? An addition to society or a contribution to humanity?

As soon as this question is answered in your life, you will never be among the losers.

A short summary of the few principles stated:

1. No matter what ranks you occupy, no one loses.
2. Sometimes the difference between a winner and a loser is only attitudinal.
3. Our mind is the centre of all victory, all success.
4. Don't compare yourself with anyone, if you do, you insult yourself.
5. Each person is unique in this life. Each individual has his or her own mission to accomplish. It is important to find your own personal legend.
6. To find one's own personal legend, one will have to ask this question, among the 6 billion human beings on earth, do I want to **be an addition of humanity or a contribution of humanity?**
7. Mistakes and failures prepare for certain success.
8. The people who contribute to society make their way very early on. They set goals. They know which path to take.
9. When you don't know which way to go, you won't get anywhere. We'll turn around and finally realize that we've come to nowhere.
10. Search, search, search until you find that power within you. That will allow you to do what only you can do better than others.

FEEDING ONE'S HUNGER

When you feel whole within yourself on all levels, physically, mentally and spiritually, you are truly healthy. This is not far away, it is within you.
Sadguru.

Chap. 11. Feeding the hunger.

''Man walks around with his hunger and...
"Appetites that he must necessarily feed.

Russel Subayi Mbaya.

To feel whole, man needs to have the perfect balance on these 4 important aspects that constitute him: **body, mind, soul, heart**.

These aspects help man to give himself value that others will be able to recognize in him.

Several events in life can cause an aspect to be affected. It may turn out that one or the other aspect is broken, either by illness, disappointment, or ignorance.

In the quest to rebuild one's life, it will be necessary to identify which part of it is valued, which needs to be rebuilt in order to fully resume one's life.

There is an autonomy program in the United States called **"Interweave solution"**. It is one of the best autonomy programs in the world.

This programme aims to improve the living conditions of global citizens by building on the improvement of their business, community and family situation.

In my capacity as **Facilitator and Ambassador of Success for the Interweave Solution Autonomy Program**, I have spent more than four consecutive years doing the rounds in the French-speaking countries of Central Africa (D.R. CONGO, Congo-Brazzaville, Cameroon) to help more than 10,000 participants improve their quality of life using the evaluation technique based on the **Wheel of Life**.

The idea was to do this exercise on the wheel of life which is essential to determine which aspect of life each candidate needed to improve in order to be balanced and feel independent.

If you are reading this book right now, after you have made peace with your past, then you have decided to update your mind, your state of mind by defining certain beliefs to add or remove in your way of doing things, the last step is to nourish your appetite now. But long before feeding them, you will have to do this exercise of identifying your needs through the **wheel of life.**

This exercise can be done at any time in your life, after any incident in your life.

The Wheel of Life will help you identify important areas of your life that need to be nurtured to rebuild your life perfectly.

To make your own wheel of life, you will have to follow 4 necessary steps:

First, determine at least 8 areas that are important in your life, these can be **sports, spirituality, couple life, children, entertainment, work life,** etc..

Second, dot the dots on each sector 1, 2, 3, 4 to 10.

Third, to rate yourself honestly on this scale of 1 to 10.

In order to determine how your wheel looks by tying the points obtained for each sector.

Wheel of life. Once you have completed the first 4 steps, you will proceed to the analysis of your result. The analysis will allow you to see that your wheel is not oval as indicated by the blue line in the picture above. By having another shape than oval, this wheel will not allow you to roll properly, i.e. there are certain aspects of your life that will need to be improved in order for you to have a balanced life.

The last step is finally to determine what actions you need to take to rebuild your life. To do this, you should develop an action plan that answers these four questions:

What are the things I need to improve?
What are the things I have to stop?
What things should I prioritize?
What are the things I can delegate?

Each person has a different wheel depending on the circumstances, personal situations and events that have happened to him or her on his or her life journey. It would be interesting to analyze the personal life wheel on a very regular basis.

But, whatever the shape of its wheel, we will realize that to feel a whole man, we need to feed the hunger of the appetites of these four entities fleeing within each of us: **body, mind, soul, and heart**.

Each sector mentioned in the wheel is directly related to a given entity.

The philosopher William George Jordan identified four great hungers for life:

"**Hunger of the body, hunger of the mind, hunger of the heart and hunger of the soul.**
They are all real; they all need to be recognized, they all need to be nurtured. »

The body is nourished by healthy food, and to get the food you will have to work and have an income.

The mind is nourished by education, instruction, accumulation of knowledge.
The heart is nourished by feelings of love, peace and joy.

In order, **the soul is nourished by the quest for spirituality**.

Employment, Education, Love, Spirituality are things that nourish man in his entirety.

1. FEEDING THE HUNGER OF THE BODY

In the process of rebuilding one's life, when we must now feed our appetite, the first aspect that must be nourished is the body.

When the appetites of the body are well nourished, all the remnants of the aspects are strengthened, man feels fulfilled and has again the strength to take his life in hand.

Healthy food is an essential part of everyone's life.

In your process of rebuilding your life, you must set yourself the goal that the need for food is no longer your primary concern.

The body is to the mind, what the vehicle is to the passenger.

The body houses the mind and all the other necessary faculties that make one called a human being.

"A holy spirit in a holy body," they say.

As I write this chapter, it must be said that famine is no longer really a concern for the people of much of Europe and North America, but the report of the World Food Programme and the World Health Organization reports that in 2019 there will be more than 820 million people, or one in nine people in the world, suffering from hunger.

Hunger is worsening in many countries where economic growth is lagging behind, particularly in middle-income countries and those heavily dependent on international commodity trade.

The annual report of UN agencies also shows that income inequality is increasing in many countries where hunger is on the rise, making it even more difficult for the poor, vulnerable or marginalized to cope with economic downturns and crises.

The fight against hunger is everyone's business. This fight is first of all individual, then family, and collective.

I am delighted in my life, I experienced famine during a troubling time in my country the DR Congo. This experience helped me to appreciate the importance of food for life and for the body. I have learned to instill in my children's minds that while they are eating, they need to remember that there are many children their age in a remote corner of Africa or South America who are starving and have nothing to eat for several days.

I was in Kinshasa during the periods after the great looting of 1991-1992, we had practically nothing left to eat at home. Everything was looted in the city. In the absence of coals, gas or electric stoves, my family used the wood from our beds that we had used as coals to prepare what little food we had been able to keep.

Due to a lack of corn, cassava, our staple food, we had resorted to mixed flour as a staple pork feed. We had a family right behind our house where there were neighbours who raised the pigs, fortunately they still had some stock that they had in store.

The same situation was repeated in 1997-1998 with the so-called war of liberation waged by the AFDL to oust the dictator Mobutu, who had been in power for 32 years.
I saw how my loving mother struggled to find us to feed her.
We had to use these pork flours, which we ate without meat or fish on the side. Luckily we had a small field of sweet potato leaves in the plot, but it couldn't last for two weeks. In the sweet potato leaf recipe, onions had taken the place of meat in this dish. We had spent more than 2 months without eating the meat or fish because the cold rooms were all looted, and the town was short of fresh food.

Sometimes we had to eat off the shelf to preserve the food. If we eat on Monday, we pass on Tuesday with just water to eat some more of this pig flour on Wednesday. We were a family of 6 children at the time.

I remember well that time of famine in our family. My parents were afraid that the sack of pork meal taken from the neighbours would end up without food while the city was still under siege, and we didn't know the outcome of the war.

From that moment on, as a child I made the decision that no matter what the situation, I would do everything I could to never miss food again for myself and my future family.

In the hierarchy established by **Abraham Maslow**, five levels of human needs are identified. The first level of human need is first of all **physiological**. Thus, food is part of these physiological needs.

Man must first earn his food and clothing security before worrying about other things.

When we are affected by a problem, a worry, an unfortunate event, we tend to deprive ourselves of nourishment for our bodies.

If you find yourself in a situation of distress, you are concerned about a problem that is eating away at you, the solution is not to deprive yourself of food.

The more we deprive ourselves of food, the more vulnerable we become to disease, the shorter our life expectancy.

Body hunger is our most conscious biological need.

It is difficult to be strong mentally, spiritually when you are deficient in time.

It's hard to feel comfortable when your belly is crying out. We can't care more about our mind than our body.

I do not intend to address issues related to nutrition, but rather how to guarantee food.

Only a job, an occupation, accompanied by an income, helps each of us to feed our body's hunger.

The fight against hunger is everyone's business. This fight is first of all individual, then family, and collective.

Every person is asked to fight poverty in order not to be a victim of hunger.

EMPLOYMENT GUARANTEES FOOD.

Employment is of paramount importance to man. It values, gives dignity, earns the respect of others, and increases self-esteem.

When I found myself seeking asylum in England, I felt my dignity on the ground, a great lack of self-respect because I had to live with the help of the state, the community and the Church. I could not buy something for myself because I was restricted from working.

Immigration provisions did not allow asylum seekers to work. I had to make do with £37.70 a week from the government. I lived like this for over three years.

With this help from the State, it is difficult to socialize, to go out and meet others and finally to integrate into the host country.

It was the first time in my life that I was in a situation where I was unemployed and humiliated like that.

I knew it would pass, it was a temporary situation, but at the same time I thought of thousands of unemployed people in the world, of their situation, their resentment, their stigmatization, their rejection in society.

This situation reminded me of a reflection made by an American prophet, **Gordon B. Hinckley** who speaks of the state of mind of an unemployed man:

"An unemployed man is of special importance because he is
Deprived of his inheritance, he is being tested as Job was, for his integrity.
While the days are extended into weeks and months and even years...
From adversity, the wound deepens; and there is a strong temptation to "curse God and then" to "curse the world.
"To die.
Economic dependence continues to ruin. It humiliates him if he is strong, ravages him...
If he's weak. Sensitive or insensitive, discouraged or indifferent, rebellious or resigned, however he is threatened by spiritual ruin; for unemployment benefit is an evil and idleness a curse. It immediately becomes the seedbed of discontent, bad thinking and strange beliefs... "
(Gordon B. Hinckley, Helping Others Take Charge, 4)

When you find yourself unemployed, you can't meet all the physiological needs described by Maslow, which are gas, water, electricity, food, clothing, rent.

Personal integrity is threatened, **discontent, injuries, bad thoughts become the lot of every day.**

As an asylum seeker, I did more understand the truth of this quote when I campaign with one group from the "REFUGEE ACTIONS" called the " Refugee Asylum Seeker Voice" (RAS Voice). We used to meet every two weeks to discuss how we could campaign and bring UK government to "lift the ban" and give asylum seekers the right to work. During our meeting, I was really touched by what the experience brought by members of the group on how they are fighting to survive without a job , some people stay in that situation for more than 10 years without any dignity in the community.

When we are not able to take care of ourselves, when we are not able to feed our hunger for the body, we will easily be carried away by ephemeral beliefs.

Sometimes, for some very special reasons, we are happy to live on unemployment benefits and other social benefits. But living continuously under this system can ruin man and make him lose his dignity.

There is no dignity in living free.

The best benefit systems are those that are given for a short term while accompanying beneficiaries to regain their dignity by becoming self-sufficient through training or coaching to gain decent work.

Whether for recipients of allowances or those who give more importance to spirituality and religion while neglecting their temporal autonomy, it is important to reread this reflection quoted above by Gordon B Hinckley.

Rebuilding his life requires a decision to take charge of himself. Most problems arise when we are not autonomous. Dependency, whatever its form, does not honour man.

If you are in a relationship, disrespect can set in, a degree of complexity can arise, harmony can be broken.

For a long time, religion perpetuated the belief that man was punished and cursed to work to eat to defile it from his forehead.

Once this thought has fled into man, he may consider work as a chore, whereas work is a blessing, an opportunity to grow, to learn, to rise, to blossom.

Find a job, create a job, keep busy, to feed the hunger in your body.

Honorable work.

There is no fixed list that determines what is accepted as honourable work. A job that suits us in terms of ability, interest, capacity and skill is an honourable job.

An honorable and challenging job is done with passion.

I followed someone telling this popular story at a conference.

This story shows what honorable work is really all about:

There were several students in one classroom who were gathered together. While they were in recess, they started talking to each other.

One brought up the subject of his father's prowess in his work and said, "My father is ***a tailor,*** *if he didn't do this job, none of your fathers were going to go out 'dressed'.*

The other child answers in turn:
"I my father is ***a taxi driver****, without him, even if your parents dressed to go out, they wouldn't get far if they didn't take my father's taxi.*

The other yells at the end and says:

"My father is more important than all of you, because he's ***a doctor****. Not far away, your parents all went to die of disease."*

And so, a shy child in the corner replied:

"My father is the most important of all, because he's ***a teacher****. Without him, none of your parents would know how to read or write.*

Who's right about all of them?

The answer is simple: They are all right.

An honorable job does more than provide income. It gives pleasure, it is done with joy.

In these little children's discussions, we can well see that honourable work is any service or product that is useful to society. It makes the environment better. It makes the world a better place through its contribution.

Of course, that an honourable job must give a man a remuneration that allows him to take care of himself, to give a better life to his people.

Only honorable work can feed the body's hunger!

In the quest to rebuild your life, find a job, or create a job of your own that will guarantee your food.

2. Feeding the hunger of the Spirit.

"Arm yourself with science to the teeth! »
SHEIKH ANTA DIOP.

Hunger of spirit is a thirst for intellectual nourishment, instruction, education and personal development.

As Richards L. Evans said, *there would be no better time than now to decide to learn, to do, to develop, to work, to improve, to produce, to increase our skills, to expand in service. Nothing comes from nothing. Nothing could ever come from nothing!* »
Richards L. Evans. (Man and Message, pp.101-102)

Learning is a lifelong process.
When we have time we must always revisit his knowledge, these skills.

Skills that were essential and indispensable in the past, some are no longer essential and indispensable today.

In order to rebuild oneself deeply, it would be important to update oneself, to do training that is in demand in the current job market.

The darkest day in life is the one in which we wait for something for nothing.

It is important to have a plan to nourish your mind on a daily basis. For me this simple 5 step method helped me to find my personal legend and nourish my spirit daily:

1. **Finding a model to** follow. It can be in any area of life. Who do you want to become in life? This question must be answered in the earliest possible stage of life.

2. **Find a close mentor who** has been successful in the same area with whom to ask questions. Today's world is open with the media, if you know how to approach people, you can have coaches, mentors who live thousands of miles away and can nourish your spirit.

3. **Attend fire corners**, fairs and conferences that talk about the job you would like to follow.

4. **Make visits to universities**, training centres and schools you plan to attend.

5. **Don't let go of any opportunity to** learn. You never stop learning.

3. Feeding the hunger of the heart.

'Guard your heart more than anything else,
"For from him come the springs of life.

Proverb 4:23

If this is the case, then one of the most essential things we can do in this life is to examine our heart carefully.

The heart is tender. It is sensitive to many influences, both beneficial and harmful. It can be hurt by people. It can be numb with sin. It can be softened by love.

Early in life we learn to protect our heart. We erect like a fence around our heart, with a door. No one can pass through the gate if we don't allow it.

Other hearts have been so wounded or numbed by scars from the past, that they are surrounded by a metal fence nearly three metres long topped with razor-sharp barbed wire. The gate is locked and has a large No Passage sign.

This kind of heart swears not to love, forgive, or show its feelings for anyone else.

If you want your reconstruction of life to be complete, consider rebuilding the state of your heart.

The heart needs to be listened to, then fed. So the complete mechanism of rebuilding the heart will be through listening and nourishing the heart.

Listen to his heart.

Quantum science does not know the past, present or future.

This science says that the heart knows the future, you can follow your heart that asks you to do something that seems to make no sense in the present, but if you are able to follow your heart, do the right thing in the present, in the future, looking back you will see as if it is a plan, your plan in fact.

It is also stated that each person has a personal internal compass. This compass resides in our heart, it contains our belief system that we all have had since birth.

This compass that resides in our heart is the whole of everything we believe, everything we don't believe, so as soon as we get stuck in life, it is the inner compass, our beliefs that will help us to resolve this blockage.

It is important to always listen to your heart.

However, the greatest suffering of men comes from where we put our hearts.

This famous scripture of the Bible reminds us in these words:

''For where your treasure is, there will your heart be'' Matthew 6:21.

It is enough to do introspection well, one will realize that the major part of our happiness, our misfortune depend on where we could have put our heart.

The heart can be placed on an object, a person, a business, a project, a relationship, etc...

For the luckiest, if your heart is put into a thriving business, you will always be joyful, if your heart is placed on a woman, a faithful man, a docile, respectful, and polite child, your heart will have fewer worries and concerns.

Just as misfortune comes for the most part when the heart is placed on perishable things, things that can undergo inflation, or that only lasts over time such as success, money, vehicles.

In human relationships, one feels very unhappy when one places one's heart on a carefree, uncaring person, that is where the expression "a heartless person" comes from.

Once, I was travelling on a public transport, an old man was sitting right next to me. He was very well dressed. From the first impression, one can say that he had no worries because he was apparently in good health.
But the further the bus went, the more I observed him and realized that he was talking to himself, he was monologizing. When he realized that I was watching him, he began to address me directly. He said, young man, I don't know if you are in a relationship, or you live alone. But I just want to tell

you that in your life avoid placing your heart in someone who takes your love for a weakness. She'll start to manipulate you because she'll understand that she's your treasure. If you are in this situation, leave her as soon as possible, and if you don't, don't ever wish it to happen to you.

Once his council is over, straight away the next station arrives, and the old man came down without me having a chance to thank him for his wonderful advice.

That's why it's important to preserve your heart. Not to put it on just any object, on just any person.

To give the best of yourself, whether in a sport, in a relationship, in a field of study or professionally, you have to do it with your heart to succeed.

People who love with their heart, who commit themselves in all that they do with their heart, are not at all weak people, but rather people who have been able to nourish their heart well, they simply have a heart in good condition, often they succeed despite the fact that they may suffer on the object of their heart.

Feed his heart.

Heart hunger is when we feel lonely, when we feel low self-esteem, when we underestimate ourselves.

It is quite easy to notice that when one is misunderstood in a communication, in the midst of misunderstandings, the shock comes directly to the heart.

When a person begins to implore comradeship, sympathy and appreciation, which in his heart he lacks, he feels a famine in his heart.

Sometimes in such situations, it is more important to impose respect rather than beg for love.

However, we find that when we seek to satisfy the hunger of our neighbour's heart, we reduce our own.

Other hearts have been so wounded or numbed by the bad memories of the past, numbed by remorse, that they are surrounded by a metal fence nearly three metres long topped with razor-sharp barbed wire. The gate is locked and has a large No Passage sign.

Notice that pride is a natural consequence of putting our heart into the things of the world. Pride quickly desensitizes our heart to spiritual impressions, to the highest sensations.

I repeat, the state of our heart has a direct effect on our sensitivity to spiritual things. We choose what we let in or not.

This truth has been well formulated in the children's book The Little Prince, by Saint-Exupéry. In the story, the Little Prince becomes friends with a fox. As they part ways, the fox confides a secret to the Little Prince, and he says:

"Here's my secret... you can only see well with your heart. The essential is invisible to the eyes. »

Today, surrounded by so much information, we might think that browsing through millions of Internet pages will give us everything we need to know. We can find good and bad information on the "web", but information alone is not enough. Sometimes you have to go deep into your heart and find the truth.

How do you feed your heart?

The heart is nourished by the rays of the sun.

The sun lights up the world. The sun allows the photosynthesis of trees and flowers.

The heart is nourished by the positive feelings we put into ourselves. This feeling illuminates our life.

The heart is nourished by love.

A hymn entitled: **"You Light the Way and Repent Divine Love" from the** music of James M. Dungan (1851-1925), based on the English text by Helen Silcott Dunan (ca. 1899), helps us to understand the blessings of a heart nourished by good feelings.

The words of this hymn are:

You light the way
And spread divine love
Thanks to the sun in your heart.

And night gives way to day
For evil flees with no return,
If there's sun in your heart.

[Chorus]
Thanks to the sun in your heart,
You are allowed to turn darkness into light.
And you live in happiness
If there's sun in your heart.

2. You bring the sweetness
Who was only holding a grudge,
Thanks to the sun in your heart.
No matter how small the effort
He'll be a treasure for you,
If there's sunshine in your heart.

[Chorus]

3. And when your neighbor suffers,
You can do so much good
Thanks to the sun in your heart.
His burden will be lighter,
For he will have your help,
If there's sunshine in your heart.

[Chorus]

4. Finally you can be happy
In this world full of envious people
Thanks to the sun in your heart.
And your heart will always be
Filled with divine love,
If there's sunshine in your heart.

Thus, we see that a heart filled with sunshine can spread love around. A heart that has good feelings can change negative situations into positive situations, it is enough to have a willing heart.

A heart that has sunshine can bring sweetness to what was only resentment. It is important to probe one's heart, to see that it is necessary to forgive in order to rebuild one's life. We cannot start a new life without forgiving and forgiving ourselves. The new life that we want to rebuild must be a life without resentment.

In the newly rebuilt life, when the heart is nourished with positive feelings, it would be easy to come to the aid of those around us.

We don't live in isolation. We are part of a community, a family, a neighbourhood. We have to make a decision to be a better parent, neighbor, husband, child. It is possible to be that only by having a heart filled with sunshine and love.

It is important to rebuild one's life by nourishing one's heart with new feelings, being willing to forgive, to serve, to share.
Only a heart full of sunshine and love can do that.

Love is the greatest force in the world.

Arthur Henry King said, "Love is not just a strong emotion, not just a strong feeling. It is a driving force. It sustains us throughout our life of joyful duty" (The abundance of the Heart, Salt Lake City, Bookcraft, 1986, p.84).

In the pure heart there is no place for personal judgements and hatred, it is filled with tenderness and love, it sees no evil and only when men succeed in seeing no evil in others will they be freed from sorrow and suffering.

Purify your heart and you will make your life rich, sweet and beautiful.

4. FEEDING THE HUNGER OF THE SOUL.

''We, living beings, are infinite beings but trapped in a finite body''...
Thomas of Ansembourg.

The hunger of the soul is the burning desire to know the eternal truth. It is the burning desire of the spirit to commune with God.

It is only natural that sooner or later everyone asks themselves the question about their real identity, their mission on earth, their tour, as well as their future after their death.

Being a creature of God, he has put a small piece of his divinity in each one of us. We are called to nourish this little piece of divinity that runs within us.

The human structure is too small, stuck in the space of time, but having infinite desire, love, infinite beauty, infinite goodness, infinite tenderness.

We have to find out how to nourish these needs of the soul which are infinite parts of our being.

Everyone will have to find his or her own unique ways of doing this, which may be through prayer for believers, or through dance, yoga, spirituality, meditation, or even simple contemplation.

The Sun is the provider of energy for all, whether we are from the mineral kingdom, the vegetable kingdom, the animal kingdom or living beings, we all depend on the divine energy of the Sun, but each one connects to it in his own way.

So it's up to everyone to figure out how to get high-speed connection from this power source.

The direct consequence when our infinite parts are not nourished is depression. We get depressed, we feel suffocated, frustrated; sooner or later we can express violence.

It is not surprising to see people who do not take care to feed their infinite parts, their souls become violent in society.

I like this quotation from **Christian Singer,** which underlines that in **this world where everything is drying up, if we do not want to die of thirst, we will have to be our own source ourselves''.**

I don't want to go into too much detail on this sensitive subject of spirituality or how to nourish one's soul. Each reader will have to find it by himself.

Suffice it to say that it is simply more than essential to nourish the vital, divine parcel of life fled within us to totally rebuild our lives.

With this chapter completed, what are the principles that we should keep in mind:

1. To feel whole, man needs to have the perfect balance on these 4 important aspects that constitute him: **body, mind, soul, heart.**
2. **The Wheel of** Life **exercise will** help you identify important areas of your life that need to be nurtured to rebuild your life perfectly.
3. Employment, Education, Love, Spirituality are things that nourish man in his entirety.
4. In your process of rebuilding your life, you must set yourself the goal that the need for food is no longer your primary concern.
5. Employment is of paramount importance to man. It values, gives dignity, earns the respect of others, and increases self-esteem.
6. Hunger of spirit is a thirst for intellectual nourishment, instruction, education and personal development.
7. If you want your reconstruction of life to be complete, consider rebuilding the state of your heart. *The heart needs to be listened to, then nourished.*
8. Being a creature of God, he has put a small piece of his divinity in each one of us. We are called to nourish this little piece of divinity that runs within us.

9. Everyone will have to find his or her own unique ways of doing this, it can be prayer for believers, or these parts can be nourished by dance, yoga, spirituality, meditation, or even simple contemplation.

Resources.

Norman Vincent Peal, **When You Want You Can,** 1990.

Sun Tzu, **The Art of War**, 2008

Timothy Ferriss, **The 4-Hour Work Week**, 2007

Zoie Kaye, **Say No to Negativity,** 1999

Thomas D'ansembourg, **Stop being nice, Be true,** 2001

James Allen, **As man thinketh,** 1903.

MBS Curriculum, Interweave Solution: www.interweavesolutions.org

FSC
www.fsc.org
MIX
Papier | Fördert
gute Waldnutzung
FSC® C083411

Kolibri 360 GmbH
Ferdinand-Jühlke-Straße 7
99095 Erfurt, Deutschland
produktsicherheit@kolibri360.de

Druck:
CPI Druckdienstleistungen GmbH
im Auftrag der
Kolibri 360 GmbH
Ferdinand-Jühlke-Str. 7
99095 Erfurt